Wining and Dining

At home in Ireland

Mise en place for Salmon Ravioli (p. 54) and Breast of Chicken with Peppers (p. 40)

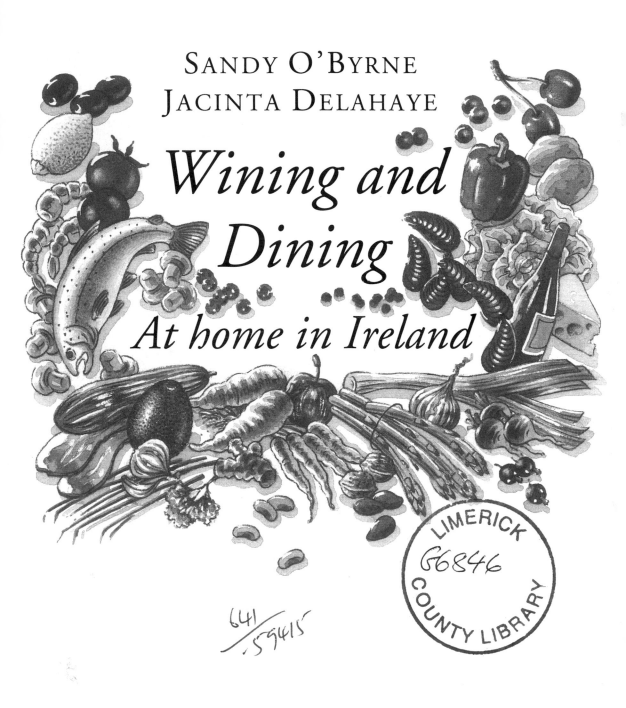

Sandy O'Byrne
Jacinta Delahaye

Wining and Dining
At home in Ireland

A. & A. FARMAR

British Library Cataloguing in Publication Data
A CIP catalogue record for this book
is available from the British Library

Cover design by Bluett
Text design and drawings by Jacques Teljeur
Photographs by John Geary
Food styling by Sandy O'Byrne and Roberto Pons
Copy-editing by Pat Carroll
Index by Helen Litton
Typesetting by A. & A. Farmar
Printing by BetaPrint

ISBN 0 9509295 9 X

Published by
A. & A. Farmar
Beech House, 78 Ranelagh Village, Dublin 6,

Contents

Introduction page 1
Equipping your Kitchen page 4
Stocks, Sauces and Other Basic Recipes page 6
How to Get the Most from Wine page 17
Guide to Wine Labels page 23
Before you start page 30

More Dash than Cash page 31
Ragoût of Seafood
Pigeon Breast with Balsamic Sauce
Baked Potatoes, Tossed Spinach
Farmhouse Cheddar Cheese
Rhubarb and Strawberry Meringue
Wines
Chardonnay (Hungary), Cabernet Sauvignon (Bulgaria)

A Taste of Italy page 38
Linguine with Mussels
Breast of Chicken with Peppers
New Potatoes with Sea Salt and Olive Oil
Parmesan Cheese with Nectarines
Almond Cake
Wines
Pinot Grigio (Italy), Barbera d'Asti (Italy), Vin Santo (Italy)

A Feast for the Eyes page 45
Sauté of Prawns with Gazpacho Sauce
Grilled Chicken Breasts with Morilles Sauce
Grated Potato Cakes, Buttered Broccoli
Selection of Goats' Cheeses
Banana Pastries with Caramel Sauce
Wines
Sancerre (France), Chianti Riserva (Italy) Orange Muscat and Flora (Australia)

Weekend Brunch page 110

Kedgeree
Baked Gammon
Stuffed Mushrooms, Breakfast Sausages
Dried Fruit Compote, Yoghurt Bowl
Breakfast Ring Cake
Wines
Cava (Spain), Riesling (Germany)

Summer Buffet page 117

Smoked Trout Mousse
Turkish Lamb and Bean Casserole
Bulghar Pilaff, Middle Eastern Salad
Summer Pudding
Wines
Vinho Verde (Portugal), Minervois (France)

Supper in the Kitchen page 123

Risotto of Sun-dried Tomatoes
Veal Baked with Rosemary
Green Salad
Gruyère Cheese
Blackcurrant Bavarois
Wines
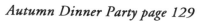
Gewurztraminer, Alsace (France), Valpolicella (Italy)

Autumn Dinner Party page 129

Scallops with Leek Noodles
Pheasant with Horseradish Sauce
Artichoke Purée, Walnut Salad
St Nectaire Cheese
Clafoutis of Plums
Wines
Orvieto Classico (Italy), Grand Cru Bourgeois (France)

Old Meets New page 137

Salmon Terrine with Chive Mayonnaise
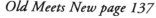
Rib of Beef with Grilled Marinated Vegetables
Aligot

Irish Cheeseboard
Fruit Strudel
Wines
Pinot Blanc (France), Shiraz (Australia)

Dinner for Vegetarians page 143

Tomato and Basil Soup
Filo Pastries with Two Sauces
Mint Sorbet
Feta Cheese en Papillote
Wild Rice Pilaff, Green Salad
Chocolate Cake
Wines
Dry Rosé (France *or* Spain), Periquita (Portugal), Banyuls (France)

Sunday Lunch page 151

Avocado Salad
Bacon en Croûte with Tarragon Sauce
Stir-fried Vegetables, Spicy Potatoes
Camembert Cheese
Hazelnut Meringue Cake
Wines
Sauvignon Blanc (Chile), Zinfandel (California)

Christmas Dinner page 157

Oysters with Spicy Sausages
Roast Stuffed Goose with Bread Sauce, Pan-fried Potatoes
Parsnip and Apple Purée, Glazed Beetroot
Gorgonzola Cheese
Christmas Pudding with Brandy Sauce
Wines
Champagne *brut* (France), Chablis (France),
Côte de Beaune Villages (France), Muscat de Beaumes-de-Venise (France)

Directory of Fine Food and Wine Suppliers in Ireland page 166
Index page 178

kindly to 'keeping warm'. With a little confidence and practice this kind of cooking becomes easy.

The old saying that you eat first with your eye is quite true. The first impression of a meal, its appearance, is a vital piece of theatre. However, you don't need a complete set of Limoges, or a large dinner service, to present food attractively—even an odd assortment of carefully blended plates and dishes can enhance the food. Good presentation does, however, mean having a knife which cuts rather than hacks, and paying attention to detail in such things as colours in a salad, properly browned pastry and carefully poured sauces.

All the menus in this book include at least one dish (usually the pudding or the vegetable) which can be prepared the day before. This is a good principle to follow, especially for formal meals. Incidentally, we would recommend trying out a new dish or method of cooking with family or close friends first. It is no fun cooking something for the first time with your boss or future in-laws sitting in the next room!

Cheese and pudding

We have chosen a cheese or cheeses for most of the menus to integrate with the rest of the meal. There is a wonderful range of cheeses available now, with many of the most interesting ones coming from producers here in Ireland. Our preference is for a small, careful selection or even a single cheese rather than the conventional 'mixture as before' cheeseboard.

We like to serve the cheese French style, before the sweet course, as this allows for different wine combinations and leads naturally into the final course. Puddings are a little special: few can resist the delicious possibilities of sweetness and texture which 'give delight and hurt not'.

Choosing the wines

Wine accompanying a meal should be the 'second sauce' to a dish and that means a taste which harmonises, refreshes or brilliantly contrasts with the food. Our aim is to help you to choose appropriate wines for particular dishes, perhaps stimulating excursions outside the well-trodden paths. This does not necessarily mean the best or the most expensive—it is a question of matching tastes. When food and wine 'marry' well, memorable meals result.

When combining food and wine, there are certain principles to remember. Most wine is mildly acidic, most food is mildly alkaline. That is the basic chemistry of the combination, and it is the reason that citrus fruits, vinegar and tomatoes, all of which have high acidity, and eggs, which have virtually none, are difficult to combine with wine.

The old rule of white wine for fish and white meat and red wine for red meat and game is generally sound; you should have a good reason for breaking it (as we do in the menu called 'Breaking the Rules'). After that, generalisations become more difficult. Broadly speaking, cabernet sauvignon wines go with lamb, yet this is hardly enough, since it immediately raises a number of questions: what kind of lamb—leg or fillet, casseroled, roast or barbecued? And what kind of cabernet sauvignon—French or Australian, young or old, oak aged or not? It is a matter of experiment and experience and in this book we hope to provide a head start on both.

The wines we have selected are those we have enjoyed with friends and have found to work well with particular dishes. We give at least two choices of wine for each course, with tasting notes, and we suggest at what age they should be drunk and the best conditions for serving. Because food tastes tend to dominate, it's a good idea to sip and taste the wines before the food, and then enjoy the combination.

Timetables

Each menu includes a preparation timetable outlining the jobs that can be done ahead and the order in which to complete them. To help make cooking more efficient and more enjoyable we have also given a number of basic recipes, a list of essential kitchen tools, shopping notes on ingredients and cook's tips, which pass on some tricks of the trade.

Remember, cooking is not an exact science. So many elements can vary—the temperature and humidity of the day, the heat of your oven, the weight of your saucepan, the freshness of your ingredients. The timetables are guidelines for cooking times, the order in which dishes should be prepared and the last-minute tasks to be done before serving. The finished dish is what counts—if the pastry is not sufficiently browned then leave it in the oven until it is just right, even if this means adding another five or ten minutes to the baking time. The dishes you cook should become your own—not exact reproductions of ours.

That's the joy of cooking, and matching food and wine—it leaves such scope for individual expression. We hope that this book will help you to enjoy entertaining and to give pleasure to your guests.

Equipping your kitchen

NOBODY SHOULD EMBARK on skilled work without the right tools. A well-equipped kitchen will save you time and endless frustration. Unfortunately, good kitchen equipment is expensive, especially knives and saucepans, but it's really not worth buying cheap utensils that wear out quickly. It's probably best to start with the basics that are essential for your style of cooking and gradually build up a range of quality cookware.

The following lists cover the cookery methods and styles contained in this book. You can select from the lists to fit your own needs; for example, if you are not interested in pastry there is no point in investing in specialised pastry-making equipment. On the other hand, if sauté dishes are your speciality it is worth buying proper pans in a range of sizes. Everyone who enjoys cooking builds up their own array of favourite tools—it's a matter of personal choice.

Knives
Preferably stainless steel
1 large chopping knife
1 ham slice
2 small paring knives
2 palette knives
1 meat filleting knife
1 fish filleting knife
1 carving fork

Stainless steel tools
2 balloon whisks
(one should be reserved for egg whites)
2 ladles
(medium and large)
1 slotted spoon
1 cooking spoon
1 cheese grater

Pots and pans

Choose sizes to suit the numbers you normally cook for, plus one or two large casseroles for buffet entertaining.

2 ovenproof sauté pans
2 small saucepans
2 medium saucepans
1 stock pot
2 enamelled cast iron casseroles *(medium and large)*
1 grill pan
1 heavy frying pan
2 non-stick frying pans
2 roasting tins

General equipment

1 kitchen scales
1 mincer
1 food processor
1 blender
1 large chopping board
2 small chopping boards
2 colanders
1 potato peeler
scissors
potato masher
bowls *(assorted sizes)*
1 sharpening steel
1 terrine dish
3 gratin dishes
12 ramekins

Pastry equipment

1 set plain round cutters
2 forcing bags
1 set plain nozzles
1 set star nozzles
1 wooden rolling pin
2 biscuit racks
2 measuring jugs
1 fine sieve
1 coarse sieve
4 plastic spatulas

Small tools

2 pastry brushes *(bristle rather than plastic)*
1 lemon squeezer
1 nutmeg grater
2 pepper mills
1 funnel
1 zester
4 wooden spoons
1 apple corer

Tins and things

1 conical sieve
2 x 8 inch (20 cm) metal flan tins
1 x 9 inch (22 cm) diameter, 2 inch (5 cm) deep, spring-form cake tin
2 x 8 inch (20 cm) sandwich tins
2 loaf tins
1 ring mould

Stocks, sauces and other basic recipes

Stocks

Home-made stock adds irreplaceable flavour to good cooking that cubes or artificial seasonings can't match. Stock made from the bones and trimmings of the meat or fish which is the main ingredient of a dish creates the best sauce, giving the true flavour of the food to the dish. When the ingredients are available make a lot of stock and freeze it in half-pint (250 ml) portions. Frozen stock will keep for three months. Unfrozen stock will keep in the fridge for three days.

All the recipes in this book assume the use of fresh herbs. The traditional *bouquet garni* consists of parsley stalks, thyme and a bay leaf. Fennel is added for fish stock, rosemary for lamb, tarragon for chicken or veal, and marjoram for most of the meat stocks.

White chicken stock

1 whole raw chicken or 3 raw carcasses (excluding the livers) or 8 raw chicken legs
3 pints (1.5 litres) water
1 large onion
1 leek
1 stick celery
12 black peppercorns
½ level tsp salt

Place the chicken in a large pot, cover with water, bring slowly to the boil.
(If using the giblets, leave out the livers.)
Skim. Add the roughly chopped vegetables and peppercorns.
Return to simmer point and cook gently for about 2 hours.
Pass through a sieve and cool.
Skim off the fat before freezing or using.
If you have used whole raw chicken the meat may be used for a salad, or any dish requiring cooked chicken.

Brown chicken stock

3 raw chicken carcasses (excluding the livers)
1 large onion
1 large carrot
1 stick celery
1 tblsp tomato purée
5 fl oz (150 ml) white wine (optional)
12 black peppercorns
3 pints (1.5 litres) water
½ level tsp salt

Chop up the carcasses (do not use the livers in the stock) and place in a roasting tin.
Roast at 210°C/gas 8 for 20 minutes or until golden.
Add the roughly chopped vegetables and roast for 5 minutes more.
Transfer to a large pot and add the tomato purée, wine, peppercorns and water.
Bring to the boil, skim and simmer for about 2 hours.
Strain the stock and cool enough to skim off the fat.
Boil rapidly to reduce by half. Cool.

Beef stock

2 lb (1 kg) chopped beef bones
1 lb (450 g) leg beef
2 large onions
2 carrots
2 sticks celery
1 sprig parsley
1 sprig thyme
1 sprig marjoram
2 tblsp tomato purée
20 black peppercorns
4 pints (2 litres) water
½ level tsp salt

Chop the beef bones into 1 inch (2 cm) pieces (or ask your butcher to do it for you).
Chop the meat roughly, into about four pieces.
Place the meat and bones in a roasting tin and brown in the oven at 210°C/gas 8 for 20 minutes or until well coloured.
Add the roughly chopped vegetables and cook for 5 minutes more.
Transfer to a large pot and add the herbs, tomato purée and peppercorns.
Cover with the water and simmer for 2 hours.
Pass through a sieve and cool.
Skim off the fat before using or freezing.

Lamb stock

2 lb (1 kg) lamb bones
1 large onion
1 carrot
3 tblsp flour
5 fl oz (150 ml) white wine
12 black peppercorns
2 tblsp tomato purée
bouquet garni with rosemary
3 pints (1.5 litres) water
½ level tsp salt

Chop the bones and place in a roasting tin.
Brown in the oven at 210°C/gas 8 for 20 minutes.
Add the roughly chopped vegetables and flour and cook for 5 minutes more.
Transfer to a large pot and add the wine, peppercorns, tomato purée, garlic and bay leaf.
Cover with the water and simmer for 1½ hours.
Pass through a sieve and cool.
Skim off the fat.
Boil rapidly to reduce by half. Cool.

Fish stock

2 lb (1 kg) bones from white fish
1 medium onion
1 leek
1 tblsp olive oil
1 sprig fennel
1 sprig parsley
5 fl oz (150 ml) white wine
12 white peppercorns
2 pints (1 litre) water
½ level tsp salt

Chop the fish bones and vegetables.
Discard any gills or black skin.
Cook gently in olive oil with the herbs for 5 minutes.
Add the wine and peppercorns and cover with the water.
Simmer for 20 minutes.
Pass through a sieve. Cool.

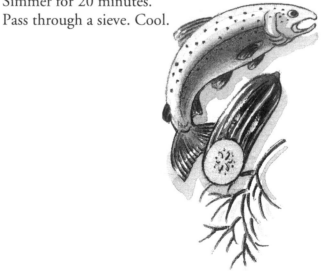

Game stock

2 lb (1 kg) trimmings
and bones from game
1 medium onion
1 carrot
1 leek
5 fl oz (150 ml) red
wine
1 sprig parsley
1 sprig thyme
1 sprig marjoram
10 juniper berries
1 tblsp tomato purée
3 pints (1.5 litres)
water
½ level tsp salt

Chop the trimmings and bones and place in a roasting tin.

Brown in the oven at 210°C/gas 8 for 20 minutes.

Add the roughly chopped vegetables and brown for 5 minutes more.

Transfer to a large pot and add the wine, herbs, juniper berries and tomato purée.

Cover with the water.

Simmer for 1½ hours.

Pass through a sieve.

Boil rapidly to reduce by half. Cool.

Tomato sauce (1)

A light fresh tomato and olive oil sauce for fish, barbecues and garnishes.

2 cloves garlic
2 lb (1 kg) ripe tomatoes
4 tblsp virgin olive oil
salt
black pepper
1 tsp sugar
12 fresh basil leaves

Peel and chop the garlic.
Peel, seed and chop the tomatoes.
Heat the olive oil and gently cook the garlic and tomatoes for 10 minutes.
Season with salt, pepper and sugar.
Stir in the torn basil leaves.
The sauce will keep in the fridge for two days or three months in the freezer.

Tomato sauce (2)

A rich sauce for pasta and meat.

2 oz (50 g) smoked
bacon (optional)
1 medium onion
2 cloves garlic
2 tblsp virgin olive oil
2 x 12 oz (350 g) cans
tomatoes
4 tblsp red wine
1 tblsp chopped fresh
basil or oregano
salt
black pepper

Roughly chop the bacon.
Peel and finely chop the onion and garlic.
Heat the oil, add the chopped ingredients and simmer for 5 minutes.
Add the tomatoes, wine, herbs and seasoning and simmer for 30 minutes.
The sauce will keep in the fridge for two days or three months in the freezer.

Breads and biscuits

Brown soda bread

1 lb (500 g) wholewheat
flour
8 oz (225 g) plain flour
5 oz (150 g) oatmeal
2 tsp salt
2 oz (50 g) butter
1 tblsp brown sugar
4 tsp bicarbonate of soda
scant 1 pint (500 ml)
buttermilk

Place the flours, oatmeal and salt in a large bowl and mix together.
Rub in the butter, then stir in the sugar and sieved bicarbonate of soda.
Pour in the buttermilk and mix lightly to a soft, but not wet, dough.
Form into one or two cakes and place on a floured baking tray.
Bake at 200°C/gas 6 for 40 minutes. You can check that the bread is ready by turning it over and tapping the bottom—if it sounds hollow it is cooked.
The bread can be frozen for three months.

Walnut and treacle bread

1¼ lb (550 g) whole-
wheat flour
1 tsp salt
1 x ¼ oz (7 g)pkt easy-
bake dried yeast
3 oz (75 g) chopped
walnuts
about ½ pint (275 ml)
water
3 tblsp black treacle

Combine the flour, salt and yeast in a mixing bowl.
Add the walnuts.
Warm the water to hand hot and mix with the treacle.
Blend into the flour mixture and stir to make a wet dough.
Spoon into a greased loaf tin.
Cover and leave to rise for about 1 hour in a warm place.
Bake at 200°C/gas 6 for 40 minutes.
You can check that the bread is ready by turning it over and tapping the bottom—if it sounds hollow it is cooked.
The bread can be frozen for three months.

White bread and rolls

This is a basic olive oil dough which can be baked in different shapes and as small rolls. The bread can also be varied by adding chopped olives, tomato purée or herbs to the dough.

1 lb (450 g) strong white flour
1 tsp salt
1 x ¼ oz (7g) pkt easy-bake dried yeast
10 fl oz (275 ml) water
3 tblsp light olive oil
flour or beaten egg to finish

Mix the flour, salt and yeast in a bowl.
Warm the water and add to the flour mixture with the olive oil.
Knead the dough vigorously for 10 minutes.
Place in a bowl, cover and leave in a warm place for 1 hour until well risen.
Shape the bread as required into cakes, long sticks or rolls and brush with egg or dust with flour.
Bake the bread at 200°C/gas 6 for 25–30 minutes.
Bake the rolls at 200°C/gas 6 for 15 minutes.
The bread and rolls are cooked when they are golden and sound hollow when tapped on the bottom.
The bread and rolls can be frozen for three months.

Wholewheat scones

8 oz (225 g) wholewheat flour
4 oz (100 g) self-raising wholewheat flour
2 oz (50 g) butter
1 tblsp brown sugar
2 tsp bicarbonate soda
1 egg
5 fl oz (150 ml) milk
beaten egg to finish (optional)

Mix the flours in a large bowl.
Rub in the butter with your fingertips.
Stir in the sugar and sieved bicarbonate of soda.
Beat the egg and combine it with the milk.
Stir into the flour to make a soft dough.
Roll out to about ¾ inch (2 cm) thick.
Cut into rounds about 2 inches (5 cm) in diameter, using a scone cutter or a strong tumbler.
If you like, brush the tops with beaten egg.
Bake on a floured baking tray at 200°C/gas 6 for 12–15 minutes.
The scones are cooked when they are well risen, golden and sound hollow when tapped on the bottom.
The scones can be frozen for three months.

Shortbread

12 oz (350 g) plain
flour
8 oz (225 g) butter
4 oz (100 g) icing sugar
caster sugar to dust

Combine the flour, butter and icing sugar either in a
food processor or with your fingertips.
Mix to a smooth dough, handling as lightly and
quickly as possible.
Chill for 30 minutes. The dough can be stored in the
fridge for 4 or 5 days or frozen.
Roll the dough to about ¼ inch (5 mm) thick and cut
into biscuits.
If you are serving shortbread with a pudding, make
the biscuits very small.
Place on a baking tray and dust with caster sugar.
Bake at 160°C/gas 3 for 10–12 minutes.
These biscuits should be eaten the day they are made.

Pastry

Pâte brisée

9 oz (250 g) plain flour
½ tsp salt
5 oz (150 g) butter
2 tsp icing sugar
1 egg
2 tblsp milk

Mix the flour and salt and spread out on the worktop
in a circle.
Chop the butter and place in the centre with the
sugar and egg.
Using a palette knife, mix together the butter, sugar
and egg to amalgamate roughly without drawing in
the flour.
Turn the palette knife so that it is perpendicular to
the worktop and chop the flour into the butter
mixture until it resembles coarse breadcrumbs and is
no longer distinct from the rest of the mixture.
Sprinkle with the milk and work quickly to a smooth
dough.
Wrap in greaseproof paper and refrigerate for at least
1 hour.
*The pastry will keep in the fridge for three to four days or
can be frozen for three months.*

Pâte sucrée

9 oz (250 g) plain flour
4 oz (100 g) butter
4 oz (100 g) icing sugar
1 egg
1 egg yolk

Spread the flour on the worktop in a circle.
Chop the butter and place in the centre with the sugar and eggs.
With a palette knife, mix the butter, sugar and eggs until roughly creamed.
Turn the palette knife so that it is perpendicular to the worktop and chop the flour into the butter mixture.
When it starts to stick together, abandon the knife and quickly work to a smooth dough with your hands.
Wrap in greaseproof paper and refrigerate for at least 1 hour.

The pastry will keep in the fridge for three to four days or can be frozen for three months.

Cook's tip: How to 'blind-bake' pastry

❝*Many recipes call for a baked pastry case to which the filling is added at a later stage. Different methods are used to blind-bake, depending on the type of pastry.*
Pâte brisée: roll out the pastry very thinly and line the tin. Press the pastry into the tin and trim the edges with a sharp knife. Prick the base of the pastry with a fork. Chill for at least 30 minutes or put in the freezer for 5 minutes. Line the base and sides of the pastry case with a single sheet of non-stick paper. Fill with beans, lentils or rice to weigh down the paper. Bake at 200°C/gas 6 for 8–10 minutes. Remove the paper, beans, etc and return to the oven for 3–5 minutes to dry the base.
Pâte sucrée: roll out the pastry very thinly and line the tin. Press the pastry into the tin and trim the edges with a sharp knife. Prick the base of the pastry with a fork. Chill for at least 30 minutes or put in the freezer for 5 minutes. Bake at 200°C/gas 6 for 5–8 minutes.❞

How to get the most from wine

READERS OF THIS BOOK do not need to be told that a glass of wine complements a meal. There are, however, ways in which the pleasure can be enhanced. This chapter shows you how to get the most out of wines. Most of the wines recommended in this book are readily available throughout the country, although some of the less well-known ones may need to be ordered in advance. (See the Directory *(pp. 166–177)* for a list of wine merchants and importers who can advise you of your nearest outlet.) We have emphasised quality at a fair price.

Wine is one of the oldest beverages known to humanity. During its history it has been treated as a necessity or as a luxury, depending on what part of the world one lived in. The challenge of this constantly evolving drink has fascinated both wine maker and wine drinker for centuries. That challenge has certainly been met over the last few decades with more progress in vine growing, wine making and wine understanding than ever before. Evidence of this is the tremendous array of wine styles available. Wine is a vast subject which can be daunting, but with a little knowledge and practice and, above all, enthusiasm, we can all learn to enhance our wine-drinking pleasure. Best of all, it can be shared with friends.

Behind every good wine there are people fired with enthusiasm, pride and a passionate love of their craft. The soil where the vine is grown, grape variety, climate, viticulture (growing the grape), vinification (conversion of grape juice into wine) and vintage each play their part. The combination of these factors, and the skill of the wine maker, determine the quality and style of individual wines.

A wine carries a vintage on the label when it has been produced from grapes harvested in the same year. Weather, as opposed to climate, is one of the most important variables influencing the quality of the vintage. A little more or less rain, frost, wind or sun can make a significant difference to the quality of the grapes and so to the wine. Some recent great Bordeaux vintages such as 1982, 1985 and 1989 are a result of near-perfect growing conditions. These wines have a structure which enables them to mature for decades. For the selected wines in this book, we have recommended the best drinking age to complement the food.

The full enjoyment of wine requires more than one sense—in fact, three. Wine should be savoured by sight, by smell and by taste, known in wine terminology as appearance, nose and bouquet. To taste wine correctly, hold the glass by the stem. This enables you to swirl the liquid in the glass and prevent it from warming up too quickly. First fill the glass with a little wine (less than a third full) and tilt it away from you against a white background. In this way, the colour of the wine won't be influenced by other colours. Whether the wine is white, red or rosé, look first for clarity. The wine should be bright, never cloudy or murky.

The second thing to look for is the type and intensity of colour. There are so many variations on a theme of colours, ranging from purple pink in young red wines to the tile, brick and garnet colours of more mature red wines. White wine is anything but white! This term encompasses a vast array of shades from water pale to straw, lush yellow and gold. The type of grape, the age of the wine, the way it is matured, with or without oak, all contribute to its colour. Fortified wines can be pale with hints of gold or deep amber and let us not forget the cheering bubbles of sparkling wine. It is also worth noting that some young white wines have a hint of spritz visible in the glass as tiny bubbles.

Some older red wines carry a sediment. This is natural and nothing to worry about. In white wine, tartrates in the form of tiny crystals may appear. These are totally harmless and are caused by the wine being subject to a sudden drop in temperature.

After the visual inspection comes the turn of the sense of smell, a critical factor in the enjoyment of wine. Swirling the wine gently round in the glass before nosing (smelling) helps it to release its secrets. The aromas (or smells) tell us if the wine is young and full of primary fruit aromas or if it has matured into something more deep and complex. The better the wine, the more subtle these sensations will be. With experience you can learn to recognise the herbaceous and cassis tones of cabernet sauvignon, the spice of syrah, the gooseberry of sauvignon, the apple or nuttiness of chardonnay and whether the wines have been influenced by oak, which imparts vanilla tones. Primary aromas in young wine are all about fruit scents while bouquet is the term used to describe wines which have matured in cask or bottle and have assumed more complex aromas often compared to animal or leather scents.

When it comes to taste there are certain elements common to all wines, whatever their colour or style. These vary in degree and intensity. Sweetness is an obvious element, its degree indicating whether the wine is dry, medium or sweet.

Acidity, particularly in white wine (think of biting into a fresh green apple or lemons and limes) is an important element as it adds freshness. Too much will make the wine appear very harsh and tart on the palate, whereas too little will make it appear dull and flabby. The fruity aspect of wine can 'attack' the palate, as in young, fruity white and red wines, be subtle when hidden by other elements, as in top-class young red wines needing time to mature, or be dried out, as in over-mature red wines. Notice how the wine feels, in other words its weight.

Finally, a substance one feels rather than tastes: tannin. This is the substance derived principally from the skins of red grapes which enables red wines to develop and age. It causes a drying feeling on the roof of the mouth, the gums, teeth and inside cheek (like the sensation of drinking cold tea). Generally, as wine matures, the tannins soften, making the wine more balanced. They eventually drop out of the wine forming a sediment, the reason that some older wines need decanting. When you swallow, try to notice how long the taste endures—the longer the 'length' of taste, the more interesting the wine.

Wine equipment

The more seriously you take wine, the more equipment you can accumulate. You will certainly need:

Corkscrews: There are literally thousands of different designs, so many indeed that they are a collectable item. Three worth considering are the Waiter's Friend, the classic sommelier's hand screw; however, it can be difficult to get used to. For ordinary use, the modern elegance of the Screwpull is hard to beat. It is easy to use, as is the wooden thread corkscrew—make sure the thread screw is strong with a very sharp tip.

Glasses: There is, believe it or not, an official International Standards Organisation (ISO) standard for a wine tasting glass. This is a clear glass, tulip shaped, about 6½ inches (16 cm) high with a stout foot to enable the glass to be held without warming the wine. These glasses are only for professional tasting—they are unsuitable for other purposes. For ordinary use, fine plain glasses are ideal. A full cupboard might consist of:

12 long-stemmed white wine glasses   12 copita glasses
12 long-stemmed red wine glasses   12 liqueur glasses
12 flute-shaped glasses   12 water tumblers
                                      6 balloon-shaped glasses

Decanters: The classic bowl shape with a narrow neck is the best type of decanter for fine wine.

Wine stoppers: These help keep wine fresh for a few hours or days. For sparkling wines, there are special stoppers to keep the 'bubble' in the bottle. In an emergency try putting the handle of a teaspoon in the neck of the bottle—it will save the sparkle for quite a few hours.

Wine savers: A squirt of this mixture of nitrogen and carbon dioxide on top of opened wine will keep the air out and maintain freshness for days.

Wine preservers: A particular favourite is the Vacu-Vin. A simple pumping action removes air from the bottle and keeps wine in good condition for up to a week.

Bottle coolers: Many styles are available. The terracotta version needs to be soaked in cold water before use. The vacuum version in plastic will keep chilled wine at the correct temperature for at least a couple of hours.

Storage

There is no mystique about storing wine; simply follow certain guidelines and your wines will rest happily until you need them. The ideal cellar has a stable temperature of between 10°C and 12°C. A gradual increase or decrease of temperature by a few degrees is much less detrimental to wine than fluctuating extremes between hot and cold. The cellar should be dark, humid and free from vibrations and odours. Odours can penetrate cork, so it is important not to store things like paint or oil near wine. Bright lights can damage wine, causing it to disintegrate very quickly. Humidity should be about 70 per cent. If the air is too dry it may cause the corks to dry out and if it is too humid may cause undesirable moulds.

There are all kinds of wine racks available and, if all else fails keep the wine in its box, but make sure it is placed on its side. This prevents the cork from drying out. The only wines which should be stored upright are fortified and sparkling wines. The alcohol of fortified wines can actually damage the cork, one of the reasons that they sometimes have screw cap closures. Storing sparkling wine upright helps prevent problems of oxidation. The wine may lose a small amount of pressure, but tests have shown that the 'fizz' tastes better.

If you are storing wine for long periods, to allow it to age in the bottle, it is a good idea to keep a record of the wines. A hard-covered book is ideal. Enter the date the wine was bought, the name of the wine, the vintage and price, and beside each wine entry leave some space for your own tasting comments.

Preparing wine for serving

If wine is served at the right temperature it will release those mysterious volatile elements that give it nose or bouquet more easily. To enable this to happen, the wine ought to be brought to the proper temperature gently and gradually without undergoing blasts of heat or cold. During this gradual warming process for fuller red wines, any sediment will be caught in the indent at the bottom of the bottle, which will make it easier to decant.

Red wine should not be hurried. Never warm the wine abruptly by standing the bottle on a hot radiator or near an open flame. The secret is to bring the wine to room temperature (between 15°C and 18°C).gently. Leave it for a few hours in the room where the meal is going to be served.

You can cool dry white wine by placing it in the door of the fridge for a few hours. The quickest method is to put it in an ice bucket with ice and water for up to ten minutes. To cool a large amount of wine quickly, freeze some bags of water, place them in a sink or large container with water, add the bottles and leave for up to ten minutes. For long, slim fluted bottles plunge neck downwards for a few minutes and then reverse.

Try to plan ahead in order to bring the wines to the proper temperature gently, thereby avoiding shocks of heat or cold. Think of the wines required for the aperitif and the meal, including starter, main course, cheese and pudding. As a rule of thumb, pale fortified wines should be served cold, while rich dark ones should be served at room temperature. More specifically, dry white and rosé wines should be served between 8°C and 12°C, light and fruity red wines between 12°C and 14°C, and full-bodied red wines should be served at room temperature, or between 15°C and 18°C. Sweet or luscious white wines and sparkling wines should be served at a temperature between 6°C and 8°C. (A wine thermometer removes the need for guesswork.)

Opening the bottle

With a sharp knife, cut the capsule covering the cork neatly just below the lip. If decanting, remove the whole capsule. Wipe around the neck of the bottle with a clean tea-towel. If the cork breaks when opening the bottle, try to get sufficient leverage by inserting the corkscrew at a sharp angle. It works nine times out of ten. As an emergency measure if the cork crumbles and looks unsightly, decant the wine through a coffee filter.

Decanting

It is not generally necessary to decant wine. In particular, it is not necessary to decant young red wines unless the cork has broken or the wine is particularly harsh, in which case pouring from one decanter to another will improve the flavour for immediate drinking.

However, sediment can form in full-bodied red wines with some age and can make the wine appear murky and unpleasant to the eye if not decanted. In addition, aerating the wine by the process of transfer from bottle to decanter develops the bouquet.

To decant your wine, cut neatly around the capsule. Remove the cork carefully. Have ready a torch or lighted candle. Don't forget that fine wines have a longer cork than ordinary wines, so a good opener is essential. With a steady hand, pour the wine from bottle to decanter, holding the lighted candle or torch to the bottle, until you see cloudiness or sediment beginning to move up the bottle. It's then time to stop. In red wines, the sediment is very fine, while in vintage port the sediment appears as a crust and can be very sludgy.

Serving

For each guest, allow one water glass and one glass for each wine being served. Remember that white wine glasses are smaller than those for red wine. Place glasses on the table in order of height, descending from left to right.

If you are serving more than one wine during the meal, the normal rules are: lighter wines before heavier; dry wines before sweet (except for certain hors-d'oeuvres); and young wines before old. In general, young wines should be served cooler than wines that have accumulated some age. If there is plenty of mineral water available, your guests will be able to clean their palates between wines.

Apart from fortified or dessert wines which are served by the half glass, you should two-thirds fill wine glasses. Any less and your guests will think you mean, any more and they won't be able to swirl the wine inside the glass and enjoy it. In general, wine bottles contain between 70 and 75 centilitres. One 75 cl bottle contains from six to eight glasses. One 75 cl bottle of sparkling wine contains about eight glasses. Fortified or dessert wines serve double the normal quantity.

Guide to wine labels

THE LABEL ON A BOTTLE OF WINE provides precise if not complete information about the contents. Certain facts, must, by law, be carried on every wine label. This bare minimum consists of:

country of origin
quantity in the bottle
the alcoholic strength
the name and address of the responsible bottler.

Most labels tell you much more, such as the wine-making region, the vintage year, if any, and possibly an indication of sweetness or dryness and the grape variety.

European wines

In their publication entitled *L'Appellation d'Origine Côntrolée* the Institut National des Appellations d'Origine des Vins et Eaux-de-Vie explains that EU regulations provide two lists of label contents. One details compulsory information, the other permissible information. The first list gives the consumer a series of objective facts, the second attempts to protect the purchaser against sales 'hype' and to limit the wording to useful information.

The EU regulations have been interpreted differently in different countries:

France: Appellation Côntrolée (AC) or Appellation d'Origine Côntrolée (AOC) is the highest quality category of French wines. The laws governing the production of these wines are strict and cover permitted grape varieties, minimum alcohol content, maximum yield, method of cultivation, method of pruning, method of vinification and even conditions of stocking and ageing. To achieve AOC status, wines are submitted to a chemical and tasting examination. Other European countries have fashioned their own quality regulations on this system.

Label terms

Brut	Very dry
Sec	Dry
Demi sec	Medium dry
Doux	Sweet
Pétillant	Slightly sparkling
Mousseux or Crémant	Sparkling
VDN	Vin doux naturel
Vin de Table	Non-vintage wine for everyday drinking
Vin de Pays	Regional or country wine
VDQS	A quality designation now being phased out
AC or AOC	Appellation Côntrolée (see above)
Grand Cru	'Great growth'—indicates an outstanding wine
Négociant	Shipper or wine merchant

Italy: The highest quality status of Italian wines is the DOCG (Denominazione di Origine Controllata e Garantita). Only a few wines are entitled to this status; these include Asti Spumante, Barbaresco, Barolo, Brunello di Montalcino, Chianti and Vino Nobile di Montepulciano.

Below this level are the DOC (Denominazione di Origine Controllata) wines, of which there are about 250. Many excellent Italian wines are classified as Vino da Tavola (table wines) because innovative producers prefer to work outside local regulations.

Label terms

Bianco	White
Classico	Refers to the heart of the production zone
Dolce	Sweet
Riserva	A wine aged for longer than normal
Rosado	Rosé
Rosso	Red
Secco	Dry
Spumante	Sparkling
Superiore	Wine with extra alcohol, usually DOC status
Vecchio	Old
Vendemmia	Vintage

Spain: The governing body, the Consejo Regulador, issues regulations for the production of wine, and issues the Denominacion de Origen (DO), which covers the country's principal wines. A more precise category has recently been established, the DOCa (Denominacion de Origen Calificada). So far Rioja is the only wine entitled to carry this on the label.

Label terms

Bodegas	Winery
Tinto	Red
Vino de Mesa	Table wine

Portugal: The highest quality category is designated as DOC (Denominacão de Origem Controlada). RD (Regioes Demarcadas) was the official status until recently and continues to be seen on some wines.

Label terms

Garrafeira	Indicates wine from an exceptional vintage with extra ageing
Quinta	Single estate
Selo do Origem	Seal of origin on bottle neck guarantees authenticity
Reserva	Vintage wine of outstanding quality
Velho	Wines with a minimum age of three years for reds and two years for whites
Vinho de Mesa	Table wine

Germany: Quality wines carry the letters QbA (Qualitätswein eines bestimmten Anbaugebietes) on the label. QmP (Qualitätswein mit Prädikat) on the label indicates quality wines with a Prädikat or special attribute. Germany categorises its wines by the degree of ripeness of the grapes at harvest. Known as Oechsle, the levels of sweetness which appear on the label are Kabinett, Spätlese, Auslese, Beerenauslese (BA) and Trockenbeerenauslese (TBA).

Kabinett	Fully ripe grapes
Spätlese	Late harvested
Auslese	Handpicked bunches of very ripe grapes
Beerenauslese (BA)	Individually selected grapes affected by noble rot
Trockenbeerenauslese (TBA)	Individual berries that look like dried raisins producing rich honey-like wines
Eiswein	Grapes harvested and pressed while frozen; richly concentrated sweet wines are the result
Trocken	Dry
Halbtrocken	Medium dry

New World wines

The New World wine countries, meaning the USA, Australia, New Zealand, South Africa and South America, have dramatically changed people's attitudes to wine. Old world stuffiness has been replaced by dynamic wine-making from innovative wine makers. Technological advance combined with dynamism led to great strides in wine quality. Following the example of Californian producers, wines began to be described by the grape variety, a welcome innovation for most wine buyers. At the same time, New World wine makers are not tied down to stringent appellation laws. This enables them to experiment and to use their skills to maximise the potential of each harvest or vintage. All labels from New World countries contain the following information:

country of origin

volume

alcoholic strength

producer's name.

There is also often a back label, giving information regarding the style of wine, how it was made and matured, with advice on serving temperature and types of food to match it.

Australia: There is no legal appellation quality status as yet in Australia, so the following is a guide to what appears on the label. When a particular grape variety is indicated on the label the wine must be produced from at least 80 per cent of the variety mentioned. If the wine is blended from two different grape varieties they are listed in order of importance.

The same rule applies to any wine region stated on the label. If a vintage is quoted, the wine must be from at least 95 per cent of the year stated.

Until recently, Australian wine labels could be labelled with European names such as Chablis, Moselle, Burgundy, Hock. In return for freer access to European markets the Australian wine industry agreed to relinquish European wine names.

California: California is the largest wine producer in North America. There are over sixty wine-growing areas, called Approved Viticultural Areas (AVAs); these are federally approved. The use of an AVA name on a label indicates that a minimum of 95 per cent of the grapes come from that area.

Label terms

Varietal	Wine described by the name of a grape variety must be made from at least 75 per cent per cent of the named grape.
Vintage	At least 95 per cent of content must be from the stated year
Reserve, Proprietor's reserve	Wines specially selected at the winery
Blush	Rosé
Fumé blanc	Californian name for the sauvignon blanc grape
Zinfandel	A red grape native to California
White Zinfandel	A pink-tinged wine

New Zealand: New Zealand has no precise appellation control indicator as yet. The label indicates the grape variety, which must be a minimum of 75 per cent of the variety stated. Grape variety and region of origin are nearly always mentioned on the label.

Chile: Chilean wines are known principally by the name of the producer. Classic grape varieties are grown and are stated on the label. These include cabernet sauvignon and merlot for reds, and sauvignon blanc, chenin blanc and chardonnay for white. Wine-growing areas include Maipo, Aconcagua, Curico, Maule, Rapel and Bío Bío.

Before you start

Read the recipes to the end

The key to quick and unstressed cooking is getting as much as possible done in advance. If all the ingredients are just to hand when you want them, and you don't have to scrabble in the saucepan rack for the right utensil, serenity follows. So, read right through the recipes for any dishes you are about to cook. Have the ingredients and utensils neatly arrayed before you start, and note key advance activities, such as when the oven has to be pre-heated. As the old proverb had it: 'an ounce of preparation saves a pound of perspiration'.

Measures

Quantities are given in imperial and metric units. Rounding to usable quantities from one measurement system to another means that they are not equivalent. In each system the units have been balanced. This means that cooks using metric measures will produce slightly different quantities of the sauces etc., from those using imperial. You may follow either system but you should not alternate between the two in any one recipe.

Spoon measurements are based on level spoons.
Spoon quantities: 1 tsp= 5 ml 1 tblsp= 15 ml.

Black pepper

When black pepper is called for in a recipe, please use freshly ground—it really does make a difference.

MORE DASH
THAN CASH

(Serves 8)
Ragoût of Seafood
Pigeon Breast with Balsamic Sauce
Baked Potatoes
Tossed Spinach
Farmhouse Cheddar Cheese
Rhubarb and Strawberry Meringue
Wines
Chardonnay (Hungary)
Cabernet Sauvignon Reserve (Bulgaria)

Pigeon should be served rare so that the meat has a pretty rose pink colour and stays succulently moist. Here it is served with a light, sharp vinaigrette, and is accompanied by a fruity, spicy red wine. The fresh tasting, new style Chardonnay cuts through the spice of the ragoût's sauce while its acidity balances the hint of sweetness in the seafood. After the nutty crumbly cheddar accompanied by the red wine, the pudding is a delicate creamy rice with a pure fruit taste and sweet shell of meringue.

Timetable

The day before	Make the fish stock (*see page 8*).
In the morning	Blanch the spinach. Make the sauce for the fish.
	Prepare the julienne. Cook the rhubarb and rice.
	Bake the potatoes, fill and leave ready to reheat.
2 hours before	Cook the seafood.
	Prepare and bake the pastry garnishes.
	Assemble and bake the meringue.
	Brown the pigeon breasts.
15 minutes before	Warm the fish, julienne, pastries and sauce.
	Roast the pigeon breasts. Toss the spinach.

Ragoût of seafood

Make the sauce

1 scant pint (500 ml)
fish stock
3 sprigs thyme
1 in (5 cm) root ginger
1 lemon
½ tsp turmeric
1–2 tblsp sugar
4 fl oz (110 ml) white
wine
10 fl oz (275 ml) cream
salt, black pepper

Take about three-quarters of the stock.
Simmer with the thyme and ginger until reduced by half. Strain.
Peel the lemon and cut the zest into fine julienne strips.
Blanch the zest in a little boiling water and refresh under cold running water.
Put the juice of the lemon into a pan with the turmeric and sugar.
Boil for 1 minute.
Add the wine and flavoured stock and reduce to one-third.
Add the cream, season and cook for 3–5 minutes.
Reheat before serving.

Prepare the julienne

½ carrot (peeled)
½ leek
½ courgette

Cut the carrot, leek and courgette into julienne strips.
Blanch quickly in boiling water—about 1 minute.
Refresh under cold running water and cool.

Cook the seafood

1½ lb (700 g) John
Dory, or another firm
white fish
2 lb (900 g) queen
scallops, or 6 large
scallops

Skin the fish and cut into strips.
Shell and clean the scallops, including the coral.
Put the remaining stock into a large pan.
Cook the seafood (including the coral) lightly for 2–3 minutes, in batches if necessary.
Do not overcrowd the pan or the fish will break up.
Drain and reserve.

Prepare and bake the pastry garnishes

4 oz (100 g) puff pastry
flour
1 egg, beaten

On a lightly floured surface roll out the pastry very thinly.

Using the cleaned shell from a queen scallop as a template, cut the pastry into eight shells, or cut into diamond shapes.

Brush with beaten egg and score with a knife in the markings of the shell.

Chill for 30 minutes.

Bake at 200°C/gas 6 for 10 minutes.

To serve

Heat the seafood, pastries and julienne (separately) in a medium oven 170–180°C/gas 4.

Warm the sauce.

Divide the seafood and sauce between eight hot plates.

Garnish with the pastries and julienne.

Shopping tip: Nut oils

❝Nut oils are some of the most versatile ingredients to become popular recently. Walnut and hazelnut oil are the most useful and have interesting flavours. Walnut is the more robust, while hazelnut oil has greater delicacy of taste. Both perish fairly quickly and should be stored in the fridge after opening and used within six weeks. Walnut oil is especially good with smoked food, avocados and goats' cheese, while hazelnut combines well with fish and game. Almond oil is very rich in taste. It can be used with chicken or in baking.❞

Pigeon breast with Balsamic sauce

Make the sauce

3 tblsp Balsamic vinegar
2 tsp Dijon mustard
salt,. black pepper
1 clove garlic, crushed
9 tblsp olive oil
2 tsp port
2 tblsp chopped chives
2 oz (50 g) pine nuts

Whisk the vinegar with the mustard and season.
Peel and crush the garlic and add to the vinegar.
Whisk in the oil.
Add the port and chives.
Just before serving, warm the sauce and whisk in the oil. Stir in the toasted pine nuts.

Cook the pigeon breasts

8 double pigeon breasts
salt
black pepper
1 tblsp olive oil

Cut the pigeon breasts from the bone.
Cut up the remaining carcasses and reserve or freeze for stock.
Season the pigeon breasts with salt and pepper.
Heat the oil and brown the breasts.
Transfer to a baking dish and roast at 190°C/gas 5 for 6–8 minutes. Remove and leave in a warm place.

To serve

If the pigeon breasts have cooled too much, reheat briefly in a hot oven.
Slice the breasts and serve with the warmed sauce.

Baked potatoes

8 medium-sized potatoes
(King Edwards or
Golden Wonders are
good for baking)
2 oz (50 g) smoked
streaky rashers
6 spring onions

Scrub the potatoes.
Bake in the oven at 190°C/gas 5 for 45–60 minutes.
Cool slightly.
Meanwhile, dice the bacon and fry it in its own fat until crisp.
Peel and chop the spring onions.
Cut a slice from the side of each cooked potato and

1 oz (25 g) butter	scoop out the soft flesh; do not break the skin.
6 tblsp cream	Mash the potato with the butter and cream.
salt	Stir in the bacon and onions. Season to taste.
black pepper	Pile the potato mixture back into the skins, forking the top of each one.
	Place on a baking tray and bake at 200°C/gas 6 for 15 minutes.

Tossed spinach

1 lb (500 g) young spinach leaves	Wash the spinach thoroughly.
	Remove the centre stalks.
1 tblsp olive oil	Blanch in lots of boiling water. Drain and cool.
2 tsp chopped rosemary	Heat the oil in a wide pan. Toss the leaves in the hot
salt	oil for a few seconds.
black pepper	Add the rosemary, salt and pepper.
	To microwave, place the washed and trimmed leaves in a bowl, add the oil, seasoning and rosemary and cook on High for 2 minutes.

Farmhouse Cheddar cheese

Cheddar is most unfairly considered an ordinary, everyday cheese, but real farmhouse Cheddar is delicious and should have pride of place at a dinner party. Try to find a mature cheese, slightly dry and nutty flavoured, that has not been stored too cold or wrapped in plastic. Ask for a piece cut freshly from a whole drum. Serve with some oatcakes and sweet wholemeal biscuits or brown treacle bread.

Cook's tip: Baked potatoes

Potatoes baked and filled as described in this menu make a good first course for an informal meal. Other delicious flavourings include blue cheese and chives, stir-fried julienne of leeks, carrot and courgette flavoured with cumin, cooked smoked haddock, or broccoli and cottage cheese.

Rhubarb and strawberry meringue

2½ lb (1.2 kg) rhubarb	Clean and trim the rhubarb.
	Cut into 2 inch (5 cm) lengths.
4 oz (100 g) granulated sugar	Cook the rhubarb with the granulated sugar until soft but not disintegrating. Cool.
12 oz (350 g) strawberries	Hull and pick over the strawberries, removing bruised berries.
1 pint (550 ml) milk	Mix the rhubarb and the strawberries.
4 oz (100 g) short grain rice	Place the milk and rice in a saucepan.
	Add the vanilla sugar. Cover and simmer very gently for 30 minutes.
2 oz (50 g) vanilla sugar	
6 fl oz (160 ml) cream	Cool and stir in the cream.
3 egg whites	Spread the rice in a gratin dish. Cover with the fruit.
3 oz (75 g) icing sugar	Whisk the egg whites until stiff but not dry.
	Gradually whisk in the icing sugar to make a firm meringue.
	Pipe or spoon the meringue over the fruit.
	Bake at 170°C/gas 4 for 12–15 minutes. Cool.

WINES

First course: Chardonnay (Hungary)

Labels	Gyöngyös Estate, Hugh Ryman *or* Chapel Hill, Balaton-Bolgár.
Availability	Widely available.
Drink	2 years old.
Serve	Chilled.
Taste	Pale in colour with hints of lime green, these wines have scents of ripe red apple which follow through on flavour, leaving a good crisp clean finish.
Awareness	Hungary produces many good value wines. Its best-known wines are the legendary Bull's Blood and the fabled sweet Tokays. Quality is indicated on the bottle by the words 'Minöségi Bor'.

Options	Novi Pazar Chardonnay *or* Khan Krum Chardonnay, both from Bulgaria, will improve with age.

Main course and cheese course: Cabernet Sauvignon Reserve (Bulgaria)

Labels	Oriahovitza *or* Russe Region.
Availability	Widely available.
Drink	5 years old.
Serve	Open up to one hour before serving at room temperature.
Taste	Good fruit aromas suggest flavours of plum and damson. The ripe fruit is followed by a spicy finish. A good if not lengthy finish with hints of tannin giving the wine structure.
Awareness	Bulgaria produces scores of good value red and white wines. In Bulgaria wines are labelled according to the grape variety from which they are made. 'Controliran' on the label indicates high-quality wines produced from specific grape varieties from specific regions.
Options	Svischtov *or* Suhindol region.

A TASTE
OF ITALY

(Serves 8)
Linguine with Mussels
Breast of Chicken with Peppers
New Potatoes with Sea Salt and Olive Oil
Parmesan Cheese with Nectarines
Almond Cake
Wines
Pinot Grigio (Italy)
Barbera d'Asti (Italy)
Vin Santo (Italy)

The main dish in this menu has complex flavours which call for the bite of acidity of the Barbera d'Asti with its damson and plummy fruit. The slight nuttiness of the Pinot Grigio highlights the taste of the mussels in the first course while its crisp acidity cuts the buttery pasta. A good chunk of crumbly Parmesan, partnered by the Barbera, sharpens the tastebuds in preparation for a light almond cake with a creamy filling. Vin Santo, Italy's famous dessert wine, is the perfect partner.

Timetable

The day before	Marinate the peppers. Make the almond cake.
In the morning	Make the mussel sauce (do not add the butter yet).
	Prepare the chicken. Clean the potatoes.
	Cook the linguine and cover with olive oil.
	Fill the cake.
1 hour before	Prepare the dressing for the chicken.
15 minutes before	Cook the potatoes.
	Bake the chicken.
5 minutes before	Heat the linguine.
	Heat the mussel sauce and add the butter.

Linguine with mussels

Make the sauce

3 lb (1.35 kg) mussels
1 shallot
5 fl oz (150 ml) white wine
2–3 cloves garlic
4 tblsp parsley
6 sun-dried tomatoes
3 oz (75 g) butter

Scrub the mussels, discarding any that are open or damaged. Place in a large saucepan with the finely chopped shallot and wine.
Cook over a high heat until all the mussels have opened. Discard any that remain closed.
Strain the shellfish, reserving the liquid.
Cool the mussels and remove from the shells.
Boil the liquid until reduced to about a quarter pint.
Add the finely chopped garlic, finely chopped parsley, roughly chopped sun-dried tomatoes and the mussels.
Just before serving whisk in the butter.

Cook the linguine

1¼ lb (550 g) fresh linguine
salt
olive oil
Parmesan cheese

Boil the pasta in plenty of salted boiling water for 3–5 minutes, drain and serve.
If not serving immediately, rinse well and leave in cold water with 2 tablespoons of olive oil.
When ready to serve, heat the pasta in the water and oil, drain well and serve.

To serve

Mix the hot pasta with the hot sauce, and sprinkle with freshly grated Parmesan cheese.

Breast of chicken with peppers

Marinate the peppers

1 red pepper
1 green pepper
4 tblsp virgin olive oil
1 clove garlic, peeled
salt, black pepper

Grill or roast the whole peppers, ideally over an open flame, until the skins are charred. Cool.
Peel. Remove the core and seeds and slice into strips.
Mix the olive oil, finely chopped garlic and seasoning.
Add the pepper strips. Cover. Refrigerate overnight.

Prepare and bake the chicken breasts

8 boned and skinned
chicken breasts (free-
range if possible)
salt
black pepper
8 green cabbage leaves
8 large slices Parma ham

Cut a pocket in the thick part of each chicken breast, and stuff with the drained pepper strips.
Season the outside of the chicken.
Remove the tough centre core from the cabbage leaves. Drop into boiling water for 2 minutes. Drain and refresh under cold water.
Take 8 squares of tinfoil, each large enough to enclose a chicken breast. Place a cabbage leaf on each piece of foil, cover with a slice of Parma ham, and place the chicken on top.
Wrap the cabbage and ham around the chicken.
Wrap the foil around the parcels to secure everything.
Place the packets in a large gratin or roasting dish and pour in water to a depth of about half an inch (1 cm).
Bake at 190°C/gas 5 for 20 minutes.

Make the dressing

4 ripe tomatoes
6 tblsp white wine
8 tblsp virgin olive oil
2 tsp pesto

Peel, seed and chop the tomatoes.
Boil the white wine to reduce to about 4 tablespoons.
Whisk in the oil and stir in the tomatoes and pesto.
Heat through gently without cooking the tomatoes.

To serve

Serve the chicken in slices with the dressing.

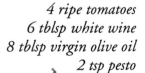

New potatoes with sea salt and olive oil

3 lb (1.5 kg) small new potatoes	Scrub the potatoes and place in a saucepan. Cover with water and bring to the boil.
1 tsp coarse sea salt	Add the salt and cook until tender—about 15
1 tblsp virgin olive oil	minutes.
1 tblsp chopped chives	Drain and sprinkle with olive oil and herbs.
2 tblsp chopped parsley	

Parmesan cheese with nectarines

Parmesan is mostly used in cooking or grated over pasta and risotto. However, its pungent taste and crumbly texture make it an interesting cheese to serve in a large chunk towards the end of a meal, especially with fruit. Look for fresh Reggiano Parmesan, the authentic Parma product. It should be stored in a cool place but not in the fridge.

Cook's tip: Marinated peppers

The marinated peppers used to stuff the chicken make a delicious dish in their own right and are a good standby. Stored in a closed jar in the fridge, the peppers will keep for ten days. For a simple salad, served with crusty bread, add some herbs to the basic olive oil and garlic marinade. A garnish of olives and anchovies or crisp streaky bacon cubes makes an interesting addition to the salad.

Almond cake

Make the cake

5 eggs	Separate the eggs. Whisk the yolks, sugar and lemon
6 oz (175 g) caster sugar	zest until thick.
grated zest of 1 lemon	Mix the finely grated carrots with the flour, then add
8 oz (225 g) carrots	to the mixture with the almonds and ginger.
2 tblsp plain flour	Whisk the egg whites until stiff but not too dry and
8 oz (225 g) ground	fold into the mixture.
almonds	Line an 8 inch (20 cm) cake tin with non-stick paper.
1 tsp ground ginger	Spoon in the cake mixture.
1 oz (25 g) pine nuts	Sprinkle the pine nuts lightly on top.
	Bake at 180°C/gas 4 for 45 minutes.
	Cool, then remove carefully from the tin.

Fill the cake

8 oz (225 g) fromage frais	Cut the cake into two layers.
	Mix the fromage frais and the caster sugar.
2–3 tblsp caster sugar	Sandwich the cake layers with the fromage frais, with
about 1 tblsp icing sugar	the pine nut layer on top.
	Dust the top with icing sugar.

WINES

First course: Pinot Grigio DOC (Italy)

Labels	Alois Lageder, Alto Adige, *or* Sterzi, Alto Adige.
Availability	Widely available,; good value.
Drink	1–2 years old.
Serve	Chilled. Open just before serving—this helps emphasise the freshness.
Taste	Notice the delicate fragrance which is reminiscent of hazelnuts. The wine is smooth on the palate with a crisp finish and slight spritz highlighting its freshness.
Awareness	Pinot Grigio produces varying styles of white wine.

Some are among Italy's finest wines, while others are bland and flavourless. Choose a reliable producer such as one of those listed above. The wines from the Friuli-Venezia Giulia region in north-east Italy are concentrated with a slightly nutty taste, while those from Trentino-Alto Adige have more structure and lasting power.

Options   If you can't find Pinot Grigio from the Alto Adige region of north-east Italy, try one from the Veneto region. A good buy is Pinot Grigio del Veneto from S. Orsola.

Main course and cheese course: Barbera d'Asti DOC (Italy)

Labels	Bersano *or* Araldica.
Availability	Specialist outlets.
Drink	3 years old.
Serve	Open at least one hour before serving at room temperature.
Taste	Observe the deep purple which can be nearly inky in colour. Before trying the wine with food give yourself a few seconds to savour the plummy flavours and note how the fruit is cut through by the bite of acidity.
Awareness	Barbera d'Asti takes its name from the grape variety (Barbera) and the name of the town (Asti) in the Piedmont region. Barbera is a very versatile grape. In Asti it produces delicious wines in an easy drinking young style. Those from around the town of Asti are especially good.
Option	Bava.

Last course: Vin Santo (Italy)

Labels	Badia a Coltibuono.
Availability	Specialist outlets.
Drink	8 years old.
Serve	Remember a little goes a long way. Serve very cool and keep in the door of the fridge.
Taste	The wonderful amber colour of the wine is a pleasure to behold. Flavours of intense apricot and honey need to be savoured and lingered over.
Awareness	Vin Santo, 'holy wine' traditionally used in religious ceremonies, is produced mainly in central Italy in Tuscany and Umbria. Harvested grapes are placed on mats or racks or hung from rafters and left to dry out. The shrivelled grapes are then pressed and the juice is placed in small barrels containing some wine from previous batches of Vin Santo. The casks are then sealed. Intermittent fermentation occurs over a period of about three years, producing wines with an alcoholic strength of 14–17 per cent. The finished style is sweet, semi-sweet or dry. This can be one of Italy's great dessert wines but some versions are crude, so it is important to buy a good example. Renowned producers include Avignonesi, Isole and Olena and Antinori.

A FEAST
FOR THE EYES

(Serves 8)
Sauté of Prawns with Gazpacho Sauce
Grilled Chicken Breasts with Morilles Sauce
Grated Potato Cakes
Buttered Broccoli
Selection of Goats' Cheeses
Banana Pastries with Caramel Sauce
Wines
Sancerre (France)
Chianti Riserva (Italy)
Orange Muscat and Flora (Australia)

Succulent fresh prawns in a sweet, spicy gazpacho sauce marry well with the fruit and zesty acidity of Sancerre. Chianti Riserva's rustic qualities are a fine match for the robust, earthy tastes of the main course. The sharp tang of goats' cheese, eaten with the Sancerre, is followed by rich banana pastries and sensational Orange Muscat and Flora.

Timetable

The day before	Marinate the vegetables for the gazpacho sauce.
	Make the chicken stock (*see page 6*).
	Make the morilles sauce. Make the caramel sauce.
In the morning	Make the gazpacho sauce. Cook the prawns.
	Make the julienne. Cook the broccoli.
	Brown the chicken. Make the potato cakes.
30 minutes hour before	Cook the chicken.
15 minutes before	Warm the gazpacho and julienne. Heat the broccoli, potato cakes and morilles sauce. Sauté the prawns.
After the main course	Bake the banana pastries.

Sauté of prawns with gazpacho sauce

Cook the prawns

3 lb (1.5 kg) fresh
prawns

Bring a large pan of water to the boil.
Add a teaspoon of salt.
Boil the prawns for 1–2 minutes. Drain and cool.
Remove the heads. Peel the prawns.

Make the gazpacho sauce

1 red pepper
2 cloves garlic
g2 ripe tomatoes
2 inch (5 cm) piece
cucumber
salt, black pepper
1–2 tsp granulated sugar
2 fl oz (55 ml) virgin
olive oil
6 fl oz (150 ml) water

Core and seed the pepper.
Peel and finely chop the garlic.
Chop the pepper, tomatoes and cucumber roughly.
Mix with the sugar, garlic and seasoning.
Cover with olive oil and leave overnight to marinate.
Blend the vegetables, marinade and water.
Pass through a sieve. Season to taste.
Before serving, heat gently. The sauce should be
warm not hot.

Make the julienne

2 small courgettes
4 basil leaves
1 clove garlic (finely
chopped)

Slice the trimmed courgettes into fine matchsticks.
Blanch in boiling water for 30 seconds. Drain.
Mix with the torn basil leaves and garlic.
Before serving, heat gently.

Sauté the prawns

4 tblsp virgin olive oil

Heat the olive oil.
Sauté the prawns quickly until lightly coloured.

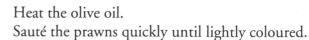

To serve

Spoon 2–3 tablespoons of warmed sauce on to each
plate. Place a little bundle of julienne in the centre.
Arrange the hot prawns around.

Grilled chicken breasts with morilles sauce

Make the mushroom sauce

16 dried morilles mushrooms (or field or button mushrooms)
5 fl oz (150 ml) white wine
6 fl oz (160 ml) chicken stock
3 tblsp Madeira (or sherry)
8 fl oz (225 ml) cream
salt, black pepper

Soak the morilles in hot water for 15 minutes.
Drain. Rinse carefully to remove any grit etc.
If using field or button mushrooms, clean and slice finely.
Boil the wine until reduced to about 6 tablespoons.
Add the stock and reduce by half.
Add the cream, mushrooms and Madeira (or sherry).
Simmer for 3–5 minutes until the flavour is concentrated.
Season to taste.

Bake the chicken

8 chicken breasts, boned and skinned
2 tblsp groundnut oil

Heat the oil on a grill pan or a heavy frying pan.
Brown the chicken breasts on the upper side only.
Place the chicken breasts on a baking tray.
Bake at 190°C/gas 5 for 20 minutes.

To serve

Slice each chicken breast and serve with 1–2 tablespoons of mushroom sauce.

Shopping tip: Morilles

❛Morilles (or morels) are delicately scented mushrooms which appear in the spring. They have a honeycomb appearance and a hollow domed head which needs to be carefully cleaned before cooking. Morilles are plentiful in France. In Ireland, they are occasionally available fresh but are more often sold dried. Soak the dried mushrooms for about fifteen minutes then drain, rinse and cook. Morilles are typically combined with poultry. They are also delicious in omelettes or with asparagus. ❜

Grated potato cakes

2 lb (1 kg) waxy potatoes
salt
black pepper
4 tblsp groundnut oil

Peel the potatoes. Grate them into a colander.
Place under running water for 2–3 minutes.
Soak in cold water for 10 minutes. Drain.
Dry very thoroughly, squeezing the potato in a cloth.
Heat the oil in a frying pan.
Take two or three 2½–3 inch (5 cm) cutters
(depending on the size of the pan) and stand in the
frying pan. Fill with the grated potato. Press the
mixture well down and remove the cutters.
Cook the potato cakes over a moderate heat until
crisp and golden—5–10 minutes. Turn the cakes and
cook on the other side until tender. Repeat until the
mixture is used up. Reserve on absorbent paper.
Reheat in a hot oven, 190°C/gas 5, for half an hour.

Buttered broccoli

2 lb (1 kg) broccoli
salt
2 oz (50 g) butter
black pepper

Cut the broccoli into small florets.
Bring some water to the boil and add salt.
Add the broccoli and cook for 5–10 minutes until just
tender.
Before serving, heat the butter and add the broccoli.
Season and toss until hot and buttery.

Selection of goats' cheeses

A selection of styles—soft, chalk-rind, ash dust, hand pressed—and shapes—tiny
crottins, pyramids, disks, cylinders—of goats' cheeses make an interesting cheeseboard with plenty of contrast in taste and texture. For the best-flavoured goats'
cheeses from France look for 'lait cru' on the label. There are now many excellent
Irish goats' cheeses on the market, including *Croghan* and *St Tola*, which are
milder in taste. Present the cheeses on a wicker or straw platter garnished with
vine leaves and accompanied by crusty bread. White wine, especially one made
from sauvignon blanc, rather than red, is nearly always best with goats' cheese.

Bananas pastries with caramel sauce

Make the caramel sauce

4 oz (100 g) granulated
sugar
4 tblsp cold water
4 tblsp hot water
10 fl oz (275 ml) cream

In a heavy pan, boil the cold water and sugar, without
stirring, to a rich golden brown.
Add the hot water and the cream.
Simmer until smooth.
Cool, then chill.

Prepare the bananas

8 small bananas
4 tblsp brown sugar
zest and juice of
½ orange
½ tsp cinnamon

Peel and chop the bananas.
Mix with the sugar, cinnamon, orange zest and juice.

Make the pastries

4 sheets filo pastry
2–3 oz (50–75 g) butter
icing sugar

Melt the butter. Lay two sheets of filo pastry on the
worktop. Brush with butter.
Cover with the remaining sheets. Brush with butter.
Cut each double sheet into four squares.
Spoon some banana on to each square.
Fold in two sides, then roll up to make a tiny strudel.
Place on a baking tray and brush with more butter.
Chill until ready to bake.
Bake at 200°C/gas 6 for 15 minutes.

To serve

Dust with icing sugar. Serve warm with the sauce.

WINES

First course and cheese course: Sancerre AOC (France)

Labels Domaine Vacheron *or* Les Greves, Moc et Baril *or* Jean Max Roger.

Availability Widely available.

Drink 2 years old.

Serve Cool. Place in the fridge door for one hour. Open immediately before serving.

Taste Sauvignon blanc based wines from the Loire are very pale with hints of green. Gooseberry aromas and flavours are the hallmarks of this crisp zingy wine with good length of flavour on the finish.

Awareness Named after the village located in the central vineyards of the Loire, the appellation of Sancerre covers red, white and rosé wines. White wines, made from sauvignon blanc, dominate. White wines are made without the influence of oak and, as usual, vineyard location and soil play an important role in the final style of wine. Soils can be chalk based, stony or contain a high percentage of clay. Red and rosé Sancerres are produced from the pinot noir grape.

Options An unusual and stunning combination with both the prawns and the goats' cheese proved to be Château de Rochemorin, André Lurton AOC Pessac-Leognan.

Main course: Chianti Riserva DOCG (Italy)

Labels Castello di Nipozzano, Chianti Rufina *or* Villa Antinori Chianti Classico *or* Villa di Vetrice, Chianti Rufina.

Availability Widely available.

Drink 4 years old.

Serve Open at least one hour before serving at room temperature.

Taste The flavours suggest black cherry with hints of chocolate. The attractive bitter twist is a hallmark of

	Chianti. It adds a delicious bite to the finish.
Awareness	Chianti is probably the best-known red wine of Tuscany, Italy. The region is divided into seven sub-zones including Chianti Rufina and Chianti Classico. Styles of wine vary from the light reds bottled in the traditional straw-wrapped flasks to the more complex riservas.
Options	Other good producers of Chianti Riserva are Castello dei Rampolla and Barone Ricasoli.

Last course: Orange Muscat and Flora (Australia)

Labels	Orange Muscat and Flora, Late Harvested, Brown Brothers.
Availability	Widely available.
Drink	2 years sold.
Serve	Chilled. Place in the fridge for two hours before serving or chill in ice and water for 10 minutes.
Taste	This low-alcohol dessert wine has golden glints with intense marmalade-type fruit aromas. Supple, with good length of flavours, the wine is never cloying on the palate.
Awareness	This wine is called after the two white grape varieties from which it is made. The orange muscat is part of the muscat family of grapes originating in south-east France. Wines made from this grape are always extremely aromatic and words such as marmalade and orange blossom are often used to describe them. Flora is a variety produced from a cross between the semillon and gewürztraminer grapes.

Rack of lamb with tapénade

FLAVOURS OF SPRING

(Serves 8)
Salmon Ravioli
Rack of Lamb with Tapénade
Courgette Gratin
Potatoes Roasted with Garlic and Herbs
West Cork Cheeses
Crème Brûlée with Rhubarb

Wines

Gavi (Italy)
Côtes du Rhône (France)

In this meal, flavours are combined to offer both harmony and contrasts. A light Gavi from Italy complements the salmon ravioli while a basic Côtes du Rhône has plenty of spicy fruit to balance the contrasting tastes of the lamb and olives. A selection of Irish farmhouse cheeses leads into the surprise at the end: a shiny-topped crème brûlée with a *bonne bouche* of poached rhubarb underneath the cream.

Timetable

The day before	Make the tapénade and the sauce for the lamb.
	Make the crème brûlée up to the point of adding the caramel.
In the morning	Make the ravioli and the courgette gratin.
3 hours before	Clean the potatoes.
1 hour before	Make the sauce for the ravioli. Brown the lamb.
30 minutes before	Cover the crème with caramel.
15 minutes before	Cook the potatoes.
	Roast the lamb. Bake the gratin.
	Cook the ravioli. Heat the sauces.

Salmon ravioli

Prepare the filling

12 oz (350 g) fresh fillet
of salmon
2 tsp salt
1 tsp sugar
1 tblsp chopped dill
8 dill sprigs for the
garnish
1 x 3 inch (8 cm) piece
cucumber
4–6 tblsp ricotta cheese
black pepper

Bone and skin the salmon fillet.
Mix the salt, sugar and dill and rub into the fish.
Wrap in cling film and leave in a cool place (not the fridge) for 2–4 hours.
Rinse quickly in cold running water, dry and cut int dice.
Chop the cucumber finely.
Mix together the cucumber, salmon and ricotta cheese.
Season with freshly ground black pepper.

Prepare the pasta dough

14 oz (400 g) flour
1½ tsp salt
3 eggs
2 tblsp olive oil
4–5 tblsp water

In a large bowl mix the flour and salt. Whisk the egg
Work the eggs, oil and water into the flour until the mixture forms a ball.
Turn out on to a floured surface and knead until the mixture forms a stiff, smooth dough; this will take about five minutes.
If you are using a food processor, place the eggs and flour in the bowl and process until the mixture start to form a ball; this will take about two minutes.
Wrap the dough in cling film and leave in a cool pla for about 30 minutes.

Make the ravioli

Cut the pasta dough into four sheets.
Roll out each piece to a very thin rectangle or put through a pasta roller to the second thinnest level.
Lay one piece of dough on the worktop.
Cover with teaspoons of the filling spaced about 1 inch (3 cm) apart.

Brush with water in between the filling.
Cover with another piece of pasta.
Repeat with the remaining pasta.
Firmly press the sheets of pasta together between the filling.
Using a fluted wheel or a knife, cut into parcels about 1½ inches (5 cm) square (or to a diameter of 1½ inches (5 cm) if round).
Press around the edges of each parcel individually to seal, making sure there is no air inside.
Leave in the fridge on a floured cloth until ready to cook.
When ready to cook, bring a large saucepan of salted water to the boil, add the ravioli and boil for 3 minutes. Drain and serve immediately.

Make the sauce

2 tblsp champagne (or white wine) vinegar
6 tblsp white wine
2 tblsp vermouth
6 oz (175 g) butter
salt
black pepper

Boil the vinegar and wine together until reduced to 2–3 tablespoons.
Add the vermouth and bring to the boil.
Whisk in the butter bit by bit.
Do not allow the sauce to boil.
Season and keep warm (*see page 11*).

To serve

Allow about four ravioli per person.
Pour over two tablespoons of sauce.
Garnish each portion with a sprig of dill.
Serve immediately.

Rack of lamb with tapénade

Make the tapénade

30 black olives	Drain, rinse and stone the olives.
15 capers	Work to a coarse purée with the capers, peeled garlic,
2 cloves garlic	anchovies and oil; this is easily done in a
6 anchovies	food processor.
2 tblsp virgin olive oil	Keep in the fridge until ready to serve.

Prepare the lamb

2 full racks of lamb,	Remove the chine bone and the tips of the ribs from
8 cutlets each	the lamb or ask your butcher to do this for you.
	Trim excess fat. Reserve meaty trimmings.

Make the sauce

lamb bones and	Chop the bones into 2 inch (5 cm) pieces.
trimmings	Place with the trimmings in a roasting tin and brown
1 medium onion	in the oven at 220°C/gas 8 for 25 minutes.
3 tblsp flour	Add the roughly chopped onion and flour and return
2 cloves garlic	to the oven for 5 minutes. Transfer the contents to a
5 fl oz (150 ml) white	large saucepan, scraping the tin well.
wine	Add the peeled garlic, wine, tomato purée, herbs,
1 tblsp tomato purée	peppercorns and 2 pints (1 litre) water. Bring to the
1 sprig rosemary	boil and skim. Simmer for 50 minutes.
1 sprig thyme	Strain, then reduce to half quantity by rapid boiling.
12 black peppercorns	Cool. Reheat just before serving.

Cook's tip: Tapénade

❝Tapénade is very easy to make in quantity, especially in a food processor. It can then be stored in sealed jars (cover the top with a film of olive oil before sealing) in the fridge for a few days. For a simple canapé, spread the mixture on toasted slices of French bread rubbed with a clove of garlic.❞

Roast the lamb

1 tblsp groundnut oil	Heat the oil in a heavy pan. Season the lamb. Brown it on the fat side in the hot oil.
salt	
black pepper	Roast for 20 minutes at 200°C/gas 6. Remove from the oven. Leave in a warm place until ready to serve.

To serve

If the lamb has cooled too much, return it to the hot oven for 2–3 minutes before serving.

Carve the lamb into cutlets and serve on warmed plates, allowing two cutlets per person, with two tablespoons of the sauce and one heaped teaspoon of tapénade. Place the dishes of vegetables on the table and let guests help themselves.

Courgette gratin

1 medium onion	Finely chop the peeled onion and garlic.
1 clove garlic	In a frying pan, heat the oil and cook the onion and garlic until golden but not brown.
3 lb (1.35 kg) courgettes	
2 tblsp chopped tarragon	Grate the courgettes and add to the pan. Stir and fry for about five minutes.
3 eggs	
6 tblsp cream	Drain in a colander and cool.
salt	Whisk the eggs, cream, seasoning and half the cheese.
black pepper	Mix with the vegetables and tarragon and pour into a gratin dish.
8 tblsp freshly grated	
Parmesan cheese	Sprinkle with the remaining cheese.
	Bake at 180°C/gas 4 for 30–40 minutes, until golden brown on top.

Potatoes roasted with garlic and herbs

3 lb (1.5 kg) small potatoes, preferably 'baby roasters'	Scrub or peel the potatoes.
10 cloves garlic	Heat the oil in an ovenproof dish or roasting tin. Add the potatoes and whole garlic cloves and toss over medium heat until well coated with oil.
3 tblsp virgin olive oil	Season generously with salt and pepper.
coarse sea salt	Add the sprigs of herbs and 4 tablespoons of water.
black pepper	Bake at 190°C/gas 5 for 40–50 minutes.
2 sprigs thyme	Pierce the potatoes to check that they are cooked.
2 sprigs rosemary	Transfer to a hot serving dish, discarding the herbs.

West Cork cheeses

Three delicious cheeses from West Cork provide a variety of tastes and textures. *Coolea*, the mildest of the three, is a Gouda-type cheese which develops flavour as it ages, but is sweet and nutty at any stage. *Gubbeen* is a semi-soft cheese made in pasteurised and unpasteurised forms. It is rich and ripe in flavour. *Durras*, a tangy, ripe cheese, has the strongest flavour of the three. Serve a handsome piece of each cheese with oat or wholegrain biscuits and bread.

Shopping Tip: Olives

❛The black olives sold in Ireland come mainly from Spain, France, Italy and Greece. They vary in size and colour: tiny Provençal olives are often jet black while larger Spanish olives may be various shades of grey. They can be bought in jars in brine or (more expensively) oil, or 'à la grecque'—rolled in oil then vacuum packed. If bought loose or in brine they are best drained, rinsed and packed in jars, then covered in olive oil. The sealed jars will keep in a cool cupboard for a year. The flavour of the olives improves and the oil is wonderful for salads.❜

Crème brûlée with rhubarb

Poach the rhubarb

2 lb (1 kg) (about 2 bunches) fresh rhubarb
3 oz (75 g) granulated sugar

Trim the rhubarb. Cut into 2 inch (5 cm) lengths. Simmer gently in a saucepan with the sugar and about 1 tablespoon of water until soft but not mushy. Cool. Divide the fruit between eight small ramekins.

Make the crème

8 egg yolks
3 oz (75 g) caster sugar
1 pint (500 ml) cream
1 vanilla pod

Whisk the egg yolks and sugar until very creamy. Heat the cream and vanilla pod to just below boiling point—do not allow to boil. Pour on to the egg yolk mixture and mix well.
Return to heat and cook gently until thick; when the mixture coats the back of the spoon it is ready.
Spoon the rich custard over the rhubarb to just below the top of each ramekin.
Cool, then chill.

Make the caramel

8 oz (225 g) granulated sugar
5 tblsp water

Not too long before serving, say two hours, place the sugar for the caramel in a heavy pan and add 5 tablespoons of water.
Cook without stirring to a rich caramel; the liquid should be golden and crystal clear.
Quickly spoon a little caramel over the custards, twisting each ramekin as you pour to give it a fine, even coating. Protect your hand with a towel as you do this—the caramel is very hot.
Reserve at cool room temperature, but not in the fridge, until ready to serve.

WINES

First course: Gavi DOC (Italy)

Labels	S. Orsola *or* Bersano *or* Pio Cesare.
Availability	Reasonably well distributed.
Drink	1–2 years old.
Serve	Very cool.
Taste	Water pale in colour, the hallmark of Gavi is subtle fruit from the cortese grape. The taste is very fresh and crisp, but with a certain weight. The flavour ends with an attractive bite of lemony acidity.
Awareness	Gavi is the famous still white wine of the Piedmont region. It is named after the town. Wines labelled 'Cortese di Gavi' are for everyday drinking, those labelled 'Gavi DOC' are of higher quality, while wines labelled 'di Gavi' are made from grapes grown in the commune of Gavi and are considered superior.

Main course and cheese course: Côtes du Rhône AOC (France)

Labels	Guigal *or* Vidal Fleury *or* P. Jaboulet Aîné.
Availability	Widely available.
Drink	3 years old.
Serve	Open one hour before serving at room temperature.
Taste	Deeply coloured, the wine has layers of concentrated fruity aromas, followed by lots of peppery spice. The fruit concentration and spiciness continue after swallowing the wine—a big generous mouthful.
Awareness	Côtes du Rhône is the basic appellation for the southern Rhône. Red wine production dominates. The principal grape varieties are grenache, cinsault, mourvèdre, carignan and syrah. These are blended wines, most of which are intended for early drinking.
Options	Coudoulet de Beaucastel *or* Domaine St Anne *or* Château d'Aigueville.

TWO'S COMPANY

(Serves 2)
Green Asparagus Feuilleté
Magret of Duck with Apple
Gratin Potatoes
Two Tone Courgettes
Brie de Meaux and Walnuts
Fresh Cherries

Wines

White Châteauneuf-du-Pape (France)
Grand Cru Classé Bordeaux (France)

Here is a meal for lovers of any and every age. Fresh asparagus is always special, particularly garnished with light pastry crusts. It combines beautifully with the strong, rich taste of white Châteauneuf-du-Pape. The main course of boned duck breasts is easy to prepare and a delicious foil to a fine cru classé from Bordeaux. Round off the meal, and the red wine, with a rich, ripe farmhouse Brie, walnuts and fresh cherries.

Timetable

The day before	Make the pastries.
	Make the sauce for the duck.
	Prepare and cook the potato gratin.
	Cook the courgettes.
In the morning	Bake the pastries.
	Cook the asparagus.
2 hours before	Make the beurre blanc with chervil.
	Brown the duck.
15 minutes before	Reheat the pastries, asparagus, potatoes and courgettes. Roast the duck.

Green asparagus feuilleté

Make the beurre blanc

beurre blanc made with 4 oz (100 g) butter (see page 11)
2 tblsp chopped chervil

Make the beurre blanc.
Add the chervil and keep warm (*see page 11*).

Make the feuilletés

flour
4 oz (100 g) puff pastry
1 beaten egg

On a floured surface, roll out the pastry very thinly, about one-eighth of an inch (4 mm) thick.
Cut into 2 diamond shapes, about 2½ inches (6 cm) long.
Place on a baking tray. Brush with beaten egg.
With the tip of a knife, score the pastry in a grid pattern, being careful not to cut right through.
Chill for half an hour.
Bake at 200°C/gas 6 for 10 minutes. Cool.
When ready to serve, slice the pastry diamonds in half to produce 2 thin diamonds in each case.
Warm for 2–3 minutes in the oven at 180°C/gas 4.

Prepare the asparagus

12 spears fresh asparagus
salt

Trim the asparagus.
Cook in boiling salted water until tender, about 7 minutes.
Drain and cool.
Reheat gently in a low oven before serving.

To serve

Place the bottom half of each pastry on a plate, cover with 6 spears of asparagus and spoon over some sauce. Cover with the top half of the pastry and spoon more sauce around the plate.

Magret of duck with apple

Make the sauce

1 cooking apple
2 tblsp granulated sugar
1 tblsp honey
2 fl oz (55 ml) white wine
5 fl oz (150 ml) chicken, duck or beef stock
salt, black pepper
1 tblsp whiskey
1 oz (25 g) butter

Peel, core and roughly chop the apple.
Place the sugar in a saucepan with 1 tablespoon of water and boil to a rich caramel.
Add the honey, chopped apple and wine.
Boil to reduce to about half.
Add the stock and simmer for 5 minutes.
Pass through a sieve.
Season. Add the whiskey.
Just before serving, whisk in the butter.

Cook the duck

1 dessert apple
2 duck breasts, boned
salt
black pepper
1 tblsp olive oil

Peel and thinly slice the dessert apple.
Brown well in a non-stick pan.
Season the duck.
Heat the olive oil.
Brown the duck in the hot oil, then roast for 6–8 minutes at 190°C/gas 5.

To serve

Slice the duck breasts and serve garnished with the apple slices and hot apple sauce.

Shopping tip: Asparagus

❝The secret with asparagus is to buy it fresh, whether local or imported. Our own home-grown asparagus makes a brief annual appearance in May and June. Look for spears which are moderately sized. Green asparagus should be about a quarter to half an inch thick at the stem, look fresh and be supple to the touch. Avoid any which show signs of withering or are woody at the cut end.❞

Gratin potatoes

6 dried ceps	Soak the ceps in hot water for 10 minutes.
2 large potatoes	Peel and finely slice the potatoes.
1 clove garlic	Peel the garlic, crush and mix with the butter.
2 oz (50 g) butter	Drain, clean and chop the ceps.
2 oz (50 g) Gruyère cheese	Grate the cheese. Mix the milk and cream.
2 fl oz (55 ml) milk	Take two individual gratin dishes and spread each with a little of the butter.
4 fl oz (110 ml) cream	Place a layer of potato in each dish, sprinkle with the ceps and cheese.

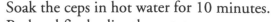

Season and dot with the remaining butter.
Continue the layers until everything is used up.
Pour over the milk and cream.
Bake at 190°C/gas 5 for 40 minutes.

Two tone courgettes

1 shallot	Peel and finely chop the shallot.
1–2 small green courgettes	Trim and dice the courgettes.
1–2 small yellow courgettes	In a saucepan, combine the shallot, coriander, seasoning, olive oil and wine.
1 tsp crushed coriander	Bring to the boil and simmer for 5 minutes.
salt, black pepper	Add the courgettes and cook for 10 minutes or until tender.
2 tblsp olive oil	
3 fl oz (75 ml) white wine	

Brie de Meaux with walnuts and fresh cherries

This is a rich, country Brie made from raw, unpasteurised milk. It is distinctive and quite delicious. Choose a piece which is ripe and creamy and serve with walnuts and fresh cherries.

WINES

First and last course: White Châteauneuf-du-Pape (France)

Labels	Chante Cigale *or* Domaine Vieux Télégraphe.
Availability	Specialist outlets—well worth seeking out.
Drink	2 years old.
Serve	Very cool but not over-chilled. Place in the door of the fridge for a few hours.
Taste	Golden in colour with fine elegant aromas of pineapples and apricots, this wine is fat and weighty on the palate with lots of fruity tones. It has a rich texture on a dry base with balancing acidity.
Awareness	Châteauneuf-du-Pape is more noted for its red than its white wines, which represent only a tiny proportion of its production. The white wine is produced from white grape varieties such as clairette, bourboulenc, roussanne, marsanne and grenache blanc. With their wonderful floral aromas backed up with good flavours and acidity, these wines are growing in popularity.
Options	From the Languedoc-Roussillon comes Mas de Daumas Gassac, a vin de pays de l'Hérault. This is a special favourite of ours.

Main course: Bordeaux Grand Cru Classé Pauillac (France)

Labels	Château Lynch-Bages *or* Château Pichon Longueville, Comtesse de Lalande.
Availability	Specialist outlets.
Drink	About 6 years old.
Serve	Open at least two hours before serving at room temperature. Older vintages, between 10 and 20 years old, should be stored upright in the dining room for a couple of days to allow sediment to settle. The bottle should be opened with care so as not to disturb the

sediment. Very old vintages, 20 to 30 years old, will benefit from the same treatment and from decanting just before serving. This helps to remove sediment and allows the wine to breathe.

Taste The appellation of Pauillac is a favourite with many Bordeaux wine lovers. The selected wines have great concentration and complex aromas which vary according to the vintage. The young, opulent plum, vanilla and cassis all 'fight' with each other in the hierarchy of aroma. As the wine develops it loses its pure fruit aromas which are replaced by complex cedar and leather scents. Do give the wine time in the glass before tasting. Inhale deeply and swirl gently. Sip the wine and allow it to reveal its secrets. Above all, linger over the taste and see how it changes when accompanied by food.

Awareness These wines all come from the commune of Pauillac in the Haut-Médoc region of Bordeaux. This commune boasts three of the five top Bordeaux wines: of the left bank: Château Latour, Château Lafite and Château Mouton-Rothschild. (The other two are Château Margaux and Château Haut-Brion.) Other top châteaux are classified as second, third, fourth and fifth growths and are known collectively as crus classé. At this level, vintage variation becomes very important as wines produced in good years have the ability to age for decades.

Options Affordable alternatives to Cru Classé are top Chilean Cabernet Sauvignon wines such as Antiguas Reservas, Cousino Macul *or* Casa Real, Santa Rita.

AFTER THEATRE SUPPER

(Serves 8)
Smoked Haddock Chowder
Wholewheat Scones
Glazed Duck
Mango Salad
Tabouleh Salad
Walnut Roulade

Wines

Sauvignon Blanc (New Zealand)
Beaujolais Cru Fleurie (France)

All you have to do to complete this meal when you arrive home with your hungry guests is heat the chowder and scones. The flavours of smoked fish and bacon in the welcoming hot soup are complemented by the aromatic fruit of the New Zealand Sauvignon Blanc. After the rich, filling first course, the cold glazed duck looks and tastes stunning. The Beaujolais Cru's smooth fruit and gentleness go well with the sweetness of the glaze, yet have enough structure to stand up to the robust meat. The finishing touch is a light sponge of ground walnuts filled with cream cheese.

Timetable

The day before	Make the chowder. Cook the duck.
	Make the tabouleh.
	Make the cake.
In the morning	Make the scones (*see page 14*).
	Make the mango salad.
	Fill the cake.
Just before serving	Reheat the chowder and add the garnish.
	Warm the scones.

Smoked haddock chowder

1½ lb (700 g) smoked haddock
3 oz (75 g) streaky rashers
12 oz (350 g) potatoes
1 onion
1 stick celery
1 pint (500 ml) milk
10 fl. oz (275 ml) fish stock (see page 8)
1½ oz (35 g) butter
7 fl oz (200 ml) cream
salt, black pepper
freshly grated nutmeg

Dice about one-third of the haddock and reserve.
Dice the bacon and fry in its own fat until crisp.
Peel and dice the potatoes.
Peel and finely chop the onion.
Trim and finely chop the celery.
Place the remaining haddock in a saucepan.
Cover with water and a dash of milk.
Bring to the boil, then drain immediately, discarding the liquid. Cut the fish into chunks.
Heat the butter and cook the finely chopped onion and celery for 5 minutes.
Add the potatoes and cook for 1–2 minutes.
Add the fish.
Add the remaining milk and the fish stock and cook for 10 minutes.
Blend to a purée. Add the cream and seasoning.

To serve

Heat the scones.
Add the diced fish and bacon to the soup and heat gently until it is hot and the fish is cooked.

Glazed duck

1 x 8 lb (3.5 kg) duck
1 dessert apple
1 onion
2 pieces star anise
1½ tblsp five spice powder
2 pints (1 litre) stout
6 oz (175 g) brown sugar
4 tblsp wine vinegar

Roughly chop the peeled apple and onion.
Mix with the star anise and 1 tablespoon of five spice powder.
Stuff the mixture into the cavity of the duck.
Combine the stout, sugar, vinegar, orange zest and juice, the remaining spice powder, soy sauce and pepper.
Prick the duck skin well and place in a roasting tin.
Pour over the stout mixture.
Roast at 180°C/gas 4 for 1½–2 hours, basting

zest and juice of 2
oranges
4 tblsp soy sauce
black pepper

frequently with the glaze.
Transfer the duck to another dish to cool, pour over the glaze and continue to baste as the duck cools, to give a dark, shining coating.

To serve
Slice thinly and arrange on a platter.

Mango salad

2–3 large, ripe mangoes
6 sprigs fresh coriander
½ red chilli
2 tblsp lemon juice
salt, black pepper
8 tblsp light olive oil

Peel and slice the mangoes.
Chop the coriander.
Remove the seeds from the chilli and chop very finely.
Sprinkle over the mangoes.
Mix the lemon juice and seasoning.
Whisk in the oil.
Pour over the mangoes.
Chill until ready to serve.

Tabouleh salad

8 oz (225 g) bulghar
1¼ pints (750 ml) hot
water
6 spring onions
2–3 cloves garlic
2 tblsp mint
4 tblsp parsley
juice of 1–2 lemons
6–8 tblsp olive oil
salt, black pepper
4 tomatoes

Soak the bulghar in hot water for about 30 minutes until the water has been absorbed and the bulghar is swollen.
Finely chop the spring onions, peeled garlic and herbs.
Stir into the bulghar with the lemon juice, olive oil and seasoning.
Peel, seed and slice the tomatoes and add to the mixture.
Serve at room temperature.

Walnut roulade

Make the cake

4 medium eggs
4 oz (100 g) caster sugar
4 oz (100 g) walnuts
2 tblsp flour

Separate the eggs. Whisk the yolks and sugar until thick. Grind the walnuts with the flour and stir into the egg yolks. Whisk the egg whites until stiff and fold in. Line a Swiss roll tin with non-stick paper and pour in the cake mixture. Bake at 200°C/gas 6 for 20 minutes. Invert the cake on to greaseproof paper and allow to cool.

Fill the cake

1 tblsp instant coffee
dissolved in 1 tblsp water
6 tblsp cream
8 oz. (225 g) cream cheese
2 tblsp caster sugar
2 tblsp brandy
1 tblsp icing sugar

Dissolve the coffee and cool. Whisk the cream lightly and whisk with the cream cheese, sugar, coffee and brandy.
Spread with the filling and roll gently, starting from a long edge.
(If you have left the unfilled cake overnight and it looks difficult to roll, cover it with greaseproof paper and a damp, warm tea towel for 15 minutes. Remove the covering and proceed.)
Dust with icing sugar and chill.

WINES

First course: Sauvignon Blanc (New Zealand)

Labels — Hunter's *or* Cloudy Bay *or* Stoneleigh, all from Marlborough.
Availability — Widely available.
Drink — 2 years old.
Serve — Chilled.
Taste — One of the appealing features of Sauvignon Blanc from New Zealand and in particular from Marlborough (South Island) is the wonderful upfront fruit, obvious in both aroma and flavour—nettles and

gooseberries simply jump out of the glass. The finish is long and crisp with zingy acidity and herbaceous bite.

Awareness	These are exciting times for wine-making in New Zealand. The white wines produced from the sauvignon blanc grape helped to establish a strong international following and this was achieved in just a few years. Cloudy Bay is perhaps the most famous of all New Zealand wines. Its sauvignon blanc wine is particularly well known and helped launch New Zealand's reputation as a quality wine-producing country.
Option	Montana

Main course: Beaujolais Cru AOC Fleurie (France)

Labels	Georges Duboeuf *or* Chauvot-Labaume *or* Faiveley.
Availability	Widely available.
Drink	3 years old.
Serve	This is one of the few red wines which benefits from being served cool, so keep it in a cool place but not the fridge. Open one hour before serving.
Taste	Fleurie is considered the most elegant and charming of the ten Beaujolais crus. Although the wine has a supple feel, it has good tannin and structure and exhibits delicious cherry liqueur flavours. Even its colour, with hints of violet, has great appeal.
Awareness	Beaujolais is produced from the gamay grape grown on granite soil. The crus come from the top villages located in the north of the region. Each Beaujolais cru is distinguished by its own individual flavours and aromas. The ten crus are: Brouilly, Côte de Brouilly, Chirobles, Chénas, Fleurie, Moulin à Vent, Morgan, Regnié, St Amour and Juliénas. All have the ability to age from 2 to 15 years depending on the vintage.
Options	Other reliable shippers of Fleurie include Drouhin, Le Piat de Beaujolais, Moreau Fontaine, Sarreau and Cellier de Samsons.

Summer barbecue

Summer Barbecue

(Serves 8)
Tagliatelle with Smoked Duck
Grilled Monkfish with Olive Oil
Green Salad
Herb Cheeses
Chocolate Ice Cream

Wines

Hunter Valley Chardonnay (Australia)
Pinotage (South Africa)

Monkfish steaks, marinated in a rich mixture of olive oil and fresh herbs, taste just as good from an indoor grill as from a barbecue, so this is a good menu for the Irish summer. Both wines go well with both the fish and the starter, the white wine blending with the richness of the pasta and highlighting the taste of the grilled fish, while the Pinotage cuts through the richness of cream and olive oil. A selection of herbed cheeses, accompanied by either wine, is followed by dark, bitter chocolate ice cream.

Timetable

The day before	Make the ice cream.
In the morning	Marinate the fish.
	Clean and chill the salad.
	Make the dressing.
	Cook the pasta and cover with olive oil and water.
One hour before	Prepare the smoked duck sauce.
15 minutes before	Drain and cook the fish.
	Heat the pasta.
	Heat the smoked duck sauce.
	Remove the ice cream from the freezer.

Tagliatelle with smoked duck

Prepare the sauce

8 oz (225 g) smoked
duck
½ oz (12 g) butter
12 fl oz (350 ml) cream
2 tblsp chopped chives
salt, pepper
4 tblsp white wine
6 tblsp freshly grated
Parmesan cheese

Cut the smoked duck into shreds. Simmer gently in butter for a minute or so.
Add the cream, chives, a little salt and freshly ground black pepper.
Simmer for 5 minutes.
Add the white wine and cheese and heat gently.

Cook the tagliatelle

1 tsp salt
2 tblsp olive oil
1 lb (500 g) fresh
tagliatelle

Bring a large pan of water to the boil, add salt, olive oil and pasta and cook for 3–4 minutes or until tender but with some bite.
Drain and serve immediately with the sauce.
If you do not want to serve the pasta at once, after draining rinse it under cold running water, put it into a bowl, barely cover with cold water and 4 tablespoons of olive oil and leave in a cool place. It will keep overnight.
When ready to serve, simply tip the contents into a saucepan, bring to the boil, drain and serve immediately with the sauce.

To serve

Mix the hot sauce with the hot pasta.
Transfer to a warm serving bowl for guests to help themselves.

Grilled monkfish with olive oil

Prepare and cook the monkfish

*16 slices of monkfish,
about 3 lb (1.5 kg) in
all, cut from the thick
part of the fish
10 tblsp virgin olive oil
5 tblsp white wine
3 tblsp fennel herb
black pepper
salt
3 ripe tomatoes
12 tblsp virgin olive oil*

Remove all the skin from the fish.
Place in a non-metal dish.
Add the olive oil, wine, chopped fennel and pepper,
turning the fish so that it is well coated.
Cover with cling film and refrigerate for 4 hours.
Drain, reserving the marinade.
Season again, this time with salt also.
If cooking outdoors, grill on the barbecue for 4
minutes each side, basting with the marinade.
If cooking indoors, grill on a grill pan on one side only.
Transfer to a baking tray, pour over the
marinade, and bake at 200°C/gas 6 for 6 minutes.
Blanch and skin and seed the tomatoes. Cut into dice.
Gently warm beside the barbecue or in a low oven.

To serve

Transfer the fish to a serving dish, or individual plates.
Spoon over the olive oil and garnish with the tomato.

Green salad

Prepare the salad and dressing

*1 butterhead lettuce
1 curly endive
1 red lettuce
1 bunch watercress
2 tblsp Balsamic vinegar
1 tsp Dijon mustard
salt, black pepper
8 tblsp virgin olive oil
1 clove garlic*

Wash and dry the lettuces and watercress.
Remove stalks from cress.
Tear the lettuce leaves into bite-sized pieces, add the
watercress and chill.
Mix the vinegar, mustard and seasoning.
Whisk in the oil.
Peel the garlic, chop into fine pieces and stir into the
dressing.
Just before serving, toss the salad with the dressing.

Herb cheeses

Herb cheeses are either marinated or wrapped in herbs, or blended with the herbs. Widely available Irish herb cheeses include *Coolea* and *Kilshanny*, hard cheeses studded with herbs and garlic, and *Boilie*, a soft, marinated variety from Ryefield Farm. Serve the cheeses on a flat straw basket, garnished with herbs and edible flowers, accompanied by wholewheat bread.

Chocolate ice cream

1 pint (450 ml) milk	Bring the milk to the boil and set aside.
3 oz (75 g) bitter chocolate	Chop the chocolate and combine with the cocoa in a bowl.
1 oz (25 g) cocoa	Pour on the hot milk and stir until smooth.
6 egg yolks	Whisk the egg yolks with the sugar.
4 oz (100 g) caster sugar	Add the hot chocolate milk and return to the saucepan.
2 tblsp chocolate liqueur (or brandy or whiskey)	Cook gently, stirring all the time, until the mixture coats the back of the spoon.
4 fl oz (100 ml) cream	Pass through a sieve into a bowl.

Cool and chill.
Add the cream and alcohol.
The alcohol is essential to this dish. It cuts the sweetness and stops the ice cream freezing too hard. However, don't add more than 2 tablespoons or it won't freeze at all.
Pour into a loaf tin or plastic carton and freeze.
Whisk up every hour or so until semi-solid, then allow to freeze hard.
Remove from the freezer about 1 hour before serving.

WINES

First, second and third courses:
Hunter Valley Chardonnay (Australia)

Labels	Rosemount Estate Show Reserve *or* Rothbury Estate.
Availability	Widely available.
Drink	2 years old.
Serve	Serve cool but not over-chilled. Place in the door of the fridge for two hours.
Taste	This wine is a delicate shade of yellow gold. The aromas suggest exotic fruit and this continues on the palate, complemented by delicate toasty flavours with tangy citrus acidity. The impact of all this fruit and oak lasts and lasts.
Awareness	Hunter Valley, in New South Wales, is famous for its quality wine-making. Chardonnay and semillon are the principal white grapes, while shiraz dominates red wine-making.

First, second and third courses:
Pinotage Wine of Origin (South Africa)

Labels	Nederburg (Paarl) *or* KWV *or* Groot Constantia.
Availability	Widely available.
Drink	4 years old.
Serve	Open an hour before serving at room temperature.
Taste	Pinotage results from crossing the red grape varieties pinot noir and cinsault. It has good quantities of jammy fruit aromas broadening out to a flavoursome mouthful with good structure.
Awareness	These wines come from the Cape, the most southerly tip of Africa. It has excellent conditions for growing cultivars such as cabernet sauvignon, pinot noir, chardonnay, sauvignon blanc and steen. Wines are made in a classic European style. Pinotage is used extensively for blended wines or in its own right.

BREAKING THE RULES

(Serves 8)
Warm Kidney and Mushroom Salad
Roasted Salmon
Cucumbers in Cream
New Potatoes with Dill
Munster Cheese
Strawberry Bande with Peach Coulis

Wines

Riesling d'Alsace (France)
St Emilion Grand Cru Classé (France)
Asti Spumante (Italy)

Red wine with fish? White wine with meat and cheese? In this menu, unusual combinations work superbly. A spicy yet fruity Riesling with bracing acidity is a fine partner for the salad of mushrooms and ginger-flavoured kidneys, while its slight honey quality works beautifully with the pungency of the Munster cheese. A Grand Cru St Emilion picks up the herby, vegetable taste of roasted salmon stuffed with fennel, its fruity dry taste matching the fish's natural sweetness. Strawberry tart, filled with a sharpish cream of soft cheese offsetting the fruit, is partnered by Asti Spumante with wonderful scents from the moscato grape.

Timetable

The day before	Make the pastry.
	Wash the salad and make the dressing.
In the morning	Stuff the salmon.
	Bake the bande and make the filling.
1 hour before	Cook the kidneys and the mushrooms.
	Bake the potatoes. Cook the cucumbers.
	Roast the salmon. Fill the bande.

Warm kidney and mushroom salad

Prepare the salad and dressing

1 oak leaf lettuce
1 radicchio lettuce
1 punnet mâché or
lambs' lettuce
2 tblsp sherry vinegar
salt
black pepper
1 tsp Dijon mustard
8 tblsp virgin olive oil
2 tsp soy sauce

Wash the salad.
Tear into bite-sized pieces.
Chill.
Mix the vinegar, seasoning and mustard.
Whisk in the oil.
Add the soy sauce.

Prepare and cook the kidneys

6 lambs' kidneys
6 oz (175 g) shitake or
button mushrooms
1 inch (2.5 cm) piece
root ginger
½ tblsp olive oil
1 clove garlic
2 tblsp dry or medium
sherry

Remove the fat from the kidneys, core and dice.
Clean the mushrooms and dice to about the same size
as the kidneys.
Cut the ginger into matchsticks.
Peel and finely chop the garlic.
Heat the oil.
Fry the kidneys and mushrooms for 3 minutes,
adding the ginger and garlic for the last minute.
Place in a gratin dish. Reserve.
Pour the sherry into the frying pan and boil up.
Transfer to a small saucepan. Reserve.
When ready to serve, gently reheat the kidney
mixture and juices.

To serve

Toss the salad with the dressing.
Divide between individual plates.
Sprinkle with the mushrooms and kidneys.
Pour a little of the sherried juices over each plate.

Roasted salmon

3 lb (1.35 kg) centre cut
salmon
1 onion
1 bulb fennel
3 oz (75 g) butter
2 tblsp parsley, finely
chopped
4 oz (100 g)
fresh breadcrumbs
salt, black pepper
juice of 1 lemon
1 egg

Clean and wipe the salmon.
Finely chop the onion and fennel. Cook in half the
butter until soft—about 10 minutes.
Add the parsley, breadcrumbs, seasoning and lemon
juice. Stir in the beaten egg, season and cool.
Season the salmon and fill with the stuffing.
Heat the remaining butter and brown the skin of the
salmon on both sides.
Roast for 15 minutes at 190°C/gas 5.
Pour in all but 4 tablespoons of the wine and cook for
15 minutes more. Place on a serving dish.
Add the remaining wine to the juices in the pan and
boil up.

To serve

Serve the salmon in slices with the wine juices poured
over.

Cucumbers in cream

2 cucumbers
1 oz (25 g) butter
2 tblsp chopped chives
salt, black pepper
8 tblsp cream

Peel the cucumbers. Cut into cubes and combine
with the butter, chives, salt and pepper.
Cover and cook for 10 minutes.
Pour in the cream and cook uncovered for 5 minutes
more. Keep warm until ready to serve.

New potatoes with dill

3 lb (1.35 kg) new
potatoes (scrubbed)
coarse sea salt
1 bunch fresh dill, about
6 sprigs
2 oz (50 g) butter

Take two pieces of foil, about 16 inches (40 cm)
square. Place half the potatoes in the centre of each.
Add the salt and dill and dot with butter.
Sprinkle each one with about 2 tablespoons of water.
Seal the foil well to make two packages.
Bake at 190°C/gas 5 for 45 minutes.

Munster cheese

Munster, the famous cheese of Alsace, is richly piquant and spicy in taste. It has an orange rind and a smooth creamy interior which should be soft but not runny. As it matures it becomes progressively stronger in taste. Serve the cheese in a large wedge accompanied by the Riesling and traditional rye bread flavoured with caraway seeds.

Strawberry bande with peach coulis

Make the pastry shell

8 oz (225 g) pâte sucrée (see page 16)
4 oz (100 g) puff pastry
1 egg, beaten

Roll the pâte sucrée to a rectangle 4 inches (10 cm) by 16 inches (40 cm). Prick with a fork.
Roll the puff pastry to a long thin rectangle.
Cut in strips, 1 inch (2.5 cm) by 18 inches (45 cm).
Brush the edges of the pâte sucrée with beaten egg and attach the strips of puff pastry to the edges.
Knock and flute the edges to join securely.
Brush the strips of puff pastry with beaten egg.
Chill for at least 30 minutes.
Bake the pastry at 200°C/gas 6 for 15 minutes.

Fill the bande

8 oz (225 g) cream cheese
6 tblsp fromage frais
3 tblsp icing sugar
1½ lb (700 g) strawberries

Whisk the cream cheese and fromage frais and sweeten lightly with a little of the icing sugar.
Spread into the cold pastry case.
Cover with the strawberries.
Sprinkle the sides with the remaining icing sugar.

Make the peach coulis

1 lb (450 g) ripe peaches
juice of 1 orange
2 tblsp sugar

Blanch and peel the peaches and chop roughly. Blend to a purée with the sugar and orange juice.
Serve with the strawberry bande.

WINES

First and cheese courses: Riesling d'Alsace AOC (France)

Labels   F. E. Trimbach *or* Alsace Willm.

Availability   Widely available.

Drink   2 years old.

Serve   Serve very cool.
Place in the fridge three hours before serving or plunge neck downwards in ice and water for eight minutes.

Taste   These wines are all about elegance with good structure. Pale with hints of green-gold, they have intense floral aromas overladen with apple fruit. Notice how the zesty acidity cuts through the fruit to leave the palate fresh and clean. Even though the flavours develop and broaden out, the wine finishes dry.

Awareness   The wines of Alsace are more often seen on restaurant wine lists than in wine shops, which is a shame. They are without doubt great food wines, equally delicious served with European and Asian foods. Most Alsace wines are white and are not influenced by oak. They are called after the grape variety from which they are produced.
As well as riesling, look out for the wines of gewürztraminer, pinot blanc, tokay pinot gris, sylvaner and muscat. Full of mouth-watering flavours, the wines have a dry finish except for the richer, sweeter styles known as 'vendange tardive' and 'selection de grains nobles'. These terms appear on the label. By law, Alsace wines must be bottled in the long slim green bottle known as 'la flûte d'Alsace'.

Option   Turckheim.

Main course: St Emilion Grand Cru Classé (France)

Labels	Château Trimoulet *or* Château Laroque.
Availability	Specialist outlets.
Drink	5 years old.
Serve	When serving red wine with fish the serving temperature is very important. Serve a little cooler than room temperature (12°C–14°C).
Taste	Before tasting the wine notice its deep colour. Wonderful woodland aromas combine with toasty overtones leached from maturation in oak.
Awareness	The wine region of Bordeaux is divided by the Dordogne and Garonne rivers into a right and a left bank which produce different styles of red and white wine. Climate, soil and grape varieties all play their part. The wines are produced from a blend of wines of different grape varieties. The left bank appellations of Médoc and Graves are dominated by cabernet sauvignon, whereas the right bank appellation St Emilion, which covers red wines only, is dominated by merlot and cabernet franc.
Options	Any one of the countless Grand Cru Classés will give great wine drinking pleasure.

Last course: Asti Spumante DOCG (Italy)

Labels	Asti Spumante Cinzano *or* Asti Spumante Martini.
Availability	Widely available.
Drink	As young as possible.
Serve	Chilled.
Taste	This sweet uncomplicated bubbly drink has all the fragrance of peachy moscato grapes. Its fruitiness tumbles out of the glass in a frothy easy to drink style.
Awareness	Italy's famous sparkling wine is made from the moscato grape from Asti in northern Italy. Its unique production process results in a naturally sweet low-alcohol sparkling wine.

GOURMET'S DELIGHT

(Serves 8)
Mousseline of Fish with Beurre Blanc
Glazed Quail
Spicy Rice Pilaff
Roquefort Cheese
Pear and Almond Tart
Wines
Muscadet de Sèvre-et-Maine *sur lie* (France)
Châteauneuf-du-Pape (France)
Sauternes 1er Cru Classé (France)

The delicate taste of the rich yet light mousseline is brought out by the yeasty Muscadet with its hint of spritz. Châteauneuf-du-Pape has the complexity needed to match the flavours in the main dish; its earthiness brings out the taste of the quail, while the fruit allows the spices to show. The contrast of the salty, tangy Roquefort and luscious sweet Sauternes is sensational, and this wine is also an ideal partner for the final pastry.

Timetable

The day before	Marinate the quail.
	Make the pilaff.
	Make the almond cream. Bake the pastry case.
	Poach the pears.
In the morning	Make the mousse.
	Fill, bake and glaze the tart.
2 hours before	Make the beurre blanc and keep warm.
1 hour before	Cook the mousse and keep warm.
	Glaze the quail.
15 minutes before	Reheat the pilaff.
	Grill the quail.

Mousseline of fish with beurre blanc

1½ lb (700 g) haddock
(or hake)
4 egg whites
1¼ pints (525 ml)
cream
salt
black pepper
butter
beurre blanc, made with
8 oz (225 g) butter
(see page 11)
2 tblsp chopped chives

Skin and bone the fish and mince very finely.
Blend the egg whites and fish.
Transfer the mixture to a bowl and place it over
another bowl filled with ice.
Gradually stir in the cream. Season to taste.
Lightly butter 8 ramekins and spoon in the mousse.
Cover each ramekin with non-stick paper and foil.
Place in a roasting tin, pour in cold water to a depth of
1 inch (2.5 cm). Cook at 160°C/gas 3 for 20 minutes.
Place a large sheet of foil over the ramekins in the tin
to keep warm, but not hot, until ready to serve.
Make the beurre blanc and add the chopped chives.

To serve

Invert the mousses on to individual plates and pour
the beurre blanc over.

Glazed quail

12 quails
12 tblsp dark soy sauce
6 tblsp dry sherry
2 tsp five spice powder
2 tblsp grated root ginger
1 tsp powdered chilli
4–6 tblsp honey
2–3 tblsp groundnut oil

Cut the quails in half through the breast bone and
right through the back.
Drop into boiling water for 1 minute. Drain.
Mix the soy sauce, sherry, five spice powder, ginger
and powdered chilli.
Add the quail, mix well and leave overnight.
Remove from the marinade and leave to drain.
Brush with honey. Leave to dry for 30 minutes.
Bake at 200°C/gas 6 for 30 minutes.
Brush with oil once or twice during cooking.

To serve

Serve three pieces of quail per person with the pilaff.
Quail must be eaten with the fingers, so provide finger
bowls and large napkins.

Spicy rice pilaff

2 pints (1 litre) chicken stock
4 tblsp groundnut oil
1 onion
3 cloves garlic
1 inch (2.5 cm) piece of root ginger
6 cardamom pods
1½ lb (700 g) long grain rice
1 fresh red chilli
2 tblsp ground coriander
4 tblsp chopped fresh coriander or parsley

Heat the stock. Finely chop the peeled onion and garlic. Chop the ginger.
Halve the chilli, remove the seeds and chop finely.
In a large saucepan heat the oil and cook the onion, garlic and ginger with the cardamom pods.
Stir in the rice and cook for 1 minute.
Add the seeded, finely chopped chilli, ground coriander and hot stock.
Cover and cook for 15 minutes.
Stir in the fresh coriander or parsley.
Serve at once or cool and reheat in the oven at 180°C/gas 4 for 15 minutes.

Roquefort cheese

This king of cheeses well deserves to be served alone as a cheese course, especially with the Sauternes. Make sure you get a piece cut from a whole drum, not a pre-packed portion. Serve the cheese on a dark wood board or deep coloured plate to bring out its texture and colours, and accompany it with water biscuits and country French bread.

Cook's tip: Roquefort cheese sauce

❛If you have some of the Roquefort left over, it makes a delicious rich sauce for steak, pork or chicken breasts.

2 oz (50 g) Roquefort
6 tblsp. white wine
4 fl oz (110 ml) cream
fresh green and black pepper
1 tsp brandy (optional)

Crumble the cheese.
Pour the wine into the pan in which the meat or chicken has been cooked. Boil to reduce by half. stirring and scraping the pan with a wooden spoon. Add cream and simmer for 2–3 minutes. Season with black pepper. Add brandy if using.❜

Pear and almond tart

Make and bake the pastry case

8 oz (225 g) pâte sucrée
(see page 16)
flour for rolling

Roll out the pastry on a lightly floured surface.
Line a 9 inch (20 cm) metal tart tin with the pastry.
Prick the base well with a fork.
Chill for 30 minutes.
Bake the pastry case for 5–10 minutes at 200°C/gas 6.
Cool.

Make the almond cream

4 oz (100 g) butter
4 oz (100 g) icing sugar
4 oz (100 g) ground
almonds
2 eggs
2 tblsp flour
2 tblsp kirsch

Cream the butter and icing sugar.
Mix in the ground almonds.
Cream again until light.
Beat in the eggs, flour and kirsch.
Chill.

Prepare the pears

6 pears
4 oz (100 g) sugar
juice of 1 lemon

Peel the pears.
Place the sugar, lemon juice and about 2 pints (1
litre) of water in a saucepan, add the pears and more
water to cover if needed.
Bring to the boil and cook until tender—10–20
minutes. Cool.

Fill and bake the tart

4–6 tblsp apricot jam

Spread the almond cream into the pastry case.
Halve the pears, remove the cores, and slice without
detaching completely at the top.
Fan slightly and arrange on top of the pastry cream.
Bake at 190°C/gas 5 for 20–25 minutes. Cool. Warm
the jam and sieve. Reheat and brush over tart.

WINES

First course: Muscadet de Sèvre-et-Maine sur lie *AOC (France)*

Labels	Château du Cléray *or* Château de la Ragotière *or* Marquis de Goulaine.
Availability	Widely available.
Drink	2 years old.
Serve	Very cool to bring out the lively freshness. Place in the door of the fridge for a few hours.
Taste	The wines have a slight minerally nose which follows through to the taste. Mixed with the fresh fruity tang of green apples is a yeasty flavour like new-baked bread. It turns into a pleasant saltiness on the finish.
Awareness	Muscadet is named after the grape from which it is made. Muscadet has three distinct appellations. One simply mentions the word 'Muscadet'. A second adds 'Sèvre-et-Maine' indicating that the wines were produced within the areas of these two tributaries of the Loire river. The third is 'Muscadet des Côteaux de la Loire', but this is seldom seen in Ireland. The words 'sur lie' indicate that the young wine was left on its own sediment up to the time of bottling. The process enhances freshness.
Option	Château de la Cassemichère.

Main course: Châteauneuf-du-Pape AOC (France)

Labels	Domaine du Vieux Télégraphe *or* Château de Beaucastel *or* Clos des Papes.
Availability	Specialist outlets.
Drink	5 years old.
Serve	Open at least two hours in advance to allow the wine to breathe at room temperature (16^{0}C–18°C).
Taste	This is in every sense a 'big' wine—intensely coloured, high in alcohol and powerful in taste and style. Its complex aromas are hard to pinpoint. Strawberry

	scents are combined with hints of spice, tobacco and even game. Rich fruit and high alcohol combine to give added weight to the wine and add complexity.
Awareness	From vineyards around the city of Avignon in the southern Rhône, red Châteauneuf-du-Pape is world famous and can be made from a blend of up to thirteen different grape varieties. The vineyards take their name from the thirteenth-century papacy of Pope Clément V at Avignon. Domaine bottled Châteauneuf-du-Pape is distinguished by the papal coat of arms embossed on the bottle.
Options	Châteauneuf-du-Pape AOC from highly respected shippers such as Jaboulet, Chapoutier, Chave, Guigal, Vidal Fleury.

Third and fourth courses: 1er Cru Classé Sauternes (France)

Labels	Château Guiraud *or* Château Coutet 1er Cru Classé (Barsac).
Availability	Specialist outlets. These wines are expensive and rare, but because of their intensity and complexity a little goes a long way.
Drink	6 years old.
Serve	Very cold. A bottle serves ten people.
Taste	Linger over the golden hues, swirl gently and see how the wine clings and eventually slides down the side of the glass in tiny rivulets. Note the concentration of rich honeyed aromas and tastes that go on and on. The wine is luscious yet held in balance by an acidity which allows the complexity to show through.
Awareness	Sauternes is the name of the wine area and appellation from the Bordeaux region. Semillon is the dominant grape variety, with some sauvignon blanc and muscadelle. When climatic conditions are right *pourriture noble* (noble rot) develops on the thin-skinned semillon grape. The grapes shrivel, concentrating the sugar. The grapes are then individually picked at their maximum sugar concentration.

Salmon mousse in pastry

CLASSIC STYLE

(Serves 8)
Salmon Mousse in Pastry with Dill Sauce
Medallions of Beef with Mushrooms
Two Vegetable Purées
Goats' Cheese Salad
Pineapple with Kirsch

Wines
Pouilly Fumé (France),
Bordeaux (France)
Armagnac (France)

The crisp acidity and aromatic fruit of Pouilly Fumé offset the richness of the salmon mousse and also complement the warm salad of grilled goats' cheese. The main dish, with its earthy mushroom sauce, is particularly good with the fruit and structure of a good Bordeaux. A refreshing end to this rich meal is pineapple with an extra bite from its natural partner, Kirsch. Follow the fruit with a digestif of fine French brandy.

Timetable

The day before	Make the mushroom sauce.
	Make the purées (leave out the cream and butter).
	Wash and chill the salad. Make the dressing.
In the morning	Prepare the mousse.
3 hours before	Cut the pineapples and chill.
	Sauté the beef. Prepare the cheese and wrap in pastry.
	Make the dill sauce and keep warm.
40 minutes before	Bake the mousse.
	Add the cream and butter to the purées and heat.
After the first course	Heat the beef and the mushroom sauce.
After the main course	Bake the cheese.

Salmon mousse in pastry with dill sauce

Prepare the mousse

*1 lb (450 g) raw fillet of
salmon
2 egg whites
14 fl oz (400 ml) cream
salt
black pepper
12 oz (350 g) puff pastry
flour
1 egg, beaten*

Chill all the ingredients and the preparation bowl.
Mince the salmon finely.
Blend in the egg whites. Place in the chilled bowl.
Gradually stir in 8 fl oz (250 ml) of the cream.
Season and chill for half an hour.
Whisk the remaining cream and fold into the mousse.
Adjust the seasoning and chill for ½ hour.
Cut the pastry in half. On a floured surface, roll each
piece very thinly—one-eighth of an inch (4 mm).
Cut an 8 inch (20 cm) circle from one piece of pastry
and a slightly larger circle from the other.
Place the smaller circle on a baking tray. Spoon the
mousse into the centre, spreading to half an inch (2
cm) from the edge, doming in the centre.
Brush the edge with beaten egg.
Cover with the other sheet of pastry. Seal the edges
well. Brush the whole with beaten egg. Cut two holes
in the pastry for the steam to escape. Chill.

Make the dill sauce

*beurre blanc (see page
11)
2 tblsp chopped dill*

Make the beurre blanc with 8 oz (225g) butter and
keep warm.
Just before serving add the dill.

Bake the mousse

Bake at 190°C/gas 5 for 35 minutes, until the pastry
is a rich golden brown.
Leave to stand for 5 minutes before serving.

To serve

Serve cut in wedges with 1–2 tablespoons of sauce.

Medallions of beef with mushrooms

Make the mushroom sauce

8 oz (225 g) oyster
mushrooms
½ oz (10 g) butter
5 fl oz (150 ml) white
wine
2 tsp Dijon mustard
4 fl oz (110 ml) beef
stock (or canned beef
consommé)
salt, black pepper

Slice the mushrooms in halves or quarters, depending on the size. Heat the butter and cook the mushrooms for 5 minutes.

Add the wine and boil rapidly to reduce by half.

Add the mustard and the stock and boil until slightly syrupy; this will take 3–5 minutes. Season to taste. Reserve. Reheat just before serving.

Note As the sauce is unthickened, it is necessary to use a good-quality stock, made with meat and bones and well reduced. If you haven't got any stock, substitute the best-quality canned consommé you can find and be careful when seasoning the sauce as the consommé may be salty.

Sauté the beef

16 x 3 oz (75 g)
medallions of fillet of
beef
salt, black pepper
1 tblsp groundnut oil

Season the beef. Heat a heavy frying pan and add the oil. Sauté the beef on a high heat for 1½–2 minutes on each side.

Take two plates, one larger than the other. Place the smaller plate upside down on the larger plate and put the medallions on this until ready to reheat. In this way the meat does not sit in its own juices and spoil. When ready to serve, place on a baking tray and reheat for 1–2 minutes in a hot oven (200°C/gas 6).

To serve

Add the meat juices to the sauce, heat and serve with the medallions.

Two vegetable purées

Make the celeriac purée

2 lb (900 g) celeriac
juice of ½ lemon
1 oz (25 g) butter
6 tblsp cream
salt, black pepper

Peel the celeriac and cut into cubes.
Place in a saucepan with salt, lemon juice and about half an inch (2 cm) of cold water. Cover and cook until tender, about 10 minutes.
Drain well and work to a purée. Add the butter and cream and season to taste.

Make the turnip purée

1½ lb (700 g) yellow
turnips (swedes)
8 oz (225 g) carrots
salt, black pepper
2 oz (50 g) butter
4 tblsp cream
freshly grated nutmeg

Peel the turnips and carrots and cut into cubes.
Place in a saucepan with salt and about 1 inch (2 cm) of water.
Cover and cook until tender, 10–15 minutes.
Drain well and mash to a purée.
Add the butter, cream, pepper and nutmeg.
When ready to serve, heat the purées gently in a low oven (160°C/gas 3) for 40 minutes, or microwave on High for about 3 minutes.
Note If you make the purées a day or two in advance, do not add the butter and cream until ready to reheat.

Cook's tip: Vegetable purée

❝A vegetable purée can be transformed into a light, elegant mousse to serve as a starter or impressive side dish. Make the purée as described, but add two whole eggs plus one egg yolk with the cream, and mix well. Butter 6–8 small ramekins and fill with the mixture. Cover and stand in a roasting tin. Pour in cold water to a depth of 2 inches (5 cm). Bake at 160°C/gas 3 for 15–20 minutes. Turn out on to warm plates and serve with beurre blanc.❞

Goats' cheese salad

Prepare the salad and dressing

1 head oak leaf lettuce
1 head radicchio
1 head frisée lettuce
2 tblsp white wine vinegar
1 tsp Dijon mustard
salt, black pepper
2 tblsp groundnut oil
6 tblsp walnut oil

Wash and dry the lettuces.
Tear into bite-sized pieces.
Chill.
Mix the wine vinegar with the mustard and seasoning.
Whisk in the oils.

Prepare the cheese

1½ lb (700 g) goats' cheese, preferably cylindrical in shape
1–2 oz (25–50 g) butter
2 oz (50 g) dried or stale breadcrumbs
salt, black pepper

Remove the rind from the cheese and cut into half-inch (2 cm) discs. Brush the cheese with melted butter, then roll in the breadcrumbs.
Place on a baking tray, season with salt and pepper and chill until ready to bake.
Bake the cheese at 200°C/gas 6 for about 8 minutes. Serve at once.

To serve

Toss the salad with the dressing. Divide between plates and top each portion with a slice of baked cheese.

Pineapple with Kirsch

2 large pineapples
6–8 tblsp icing sugar
8 tblsp Kirsch

For an illustration of this dish, *see page 160.*

Cut the pineapples into quarters lengthways, cutting right through the leaves. Cut the flesh away from the skin and detach it from the band of core down the centre. Slice the flesh like a melon, then pull the slices alternately to one side and the other from under the core. Sprinkle with icing sugar and Kirsch.

WINES

First course and cheese course:
Pouilly Fumé AOC (France)

Labels — Château de Tracy *or* De Ladoucette.
Availability — Reasonably available.
Drink — 2 years old.
Serve — Very cool. Chill for two hours in the fridge door.
Taste — Gently inhale the aromas of the wine before sipping. It will remind you of green fruits such as gooseberry with a slight smokiness. When you taste the wine the gooseberry flavour continues, but notice how the crisp acidity cuts through the fruit and the wine finishes dry.
Awareness — The Central vineyards of the Loire Valley produce France's finest examples of sauvignon blanc of which Pouilly Fumé and Sancerre are the best known wines in the area. The word 'fumé' refers to a natural white dust which settles on the underleaf of the vine. In windy weather, seen from a distance, it appears as smoke. Some people also detect a distinct smokiness in the taste of the wine. The appellation Pouilly Fumé applies only to white wines.
Options — Domaine des Berthiers, Pouilly Fumé Les Breil, or for a special occasion, Baron de L.

Main course: Bordeaux AOC (France)

Labels — Château Rabouchet *or* Château de Sours *or* Michel Lynch.
Availability — Reasonably well distributed. Specialist wine outlets.
Drink — 4 years old.
Serve — Open at least one hour before serving and serve at between 15°C and 17°C, the temperature of a moderately warm room.
Taste — Admire the wonderful garnet colour of these wines. Enjoy the aromas of cassis, cedar and vanilla before

sipping. Notice how well the flavours of the wine accompany the food.

Awareness	Bordeaux is the largest producer of fine wines in the world. AOC is the appellation applied to basic red and white wines produced anywhere within the region. Some are excellent, while others are very disappointing. Producers range from co-operatives to négociants to individual châteaux. Wines labelled 'Supérieur' have a slightly higher alcohol content.
Options	Château Bonnet *or* Château Blason-Timberlay *or* a Bordeaux Supérieur, Château Meaume.

Digestif: Armagnac (France)

Labels	Château de Labaude VSOP *or* St Vivant VSOP.
Availability	Widely available.
Drink	Ready to drink as soon as it is bottled.
Serve	Just open and serve.
Taste	Medium-sized balloon-shaped glasses make the most of Armagnac's nutty aromas and amber glints. Gentle swirling helps to concentrate the heady aromas.
Awareness	A spirit distilled from wine, Armagnac comes from Gascony, south of Bordeaux. Strict controls and legislation govern its production and maturation. The still wine is produced from white grape varieties such as ugni blanc and folle blanche in the designated growing areas of Haut Armagnac, Ténarèze and Bas Armagnac. Most Armagnacs are blends from different producers and distillers. If all the brandies in the blend are produced in the same year a vintage can be carried on the label. Single vintages must be at least ten years old before being sold. VSOP on a label indicates that the brandy is at least five years old.
Options	For an extra special occasion try a twenty-year-old or vintage Armagnac from reliable shippers such as Castarede, Janneau or Samalens.

CATCH OF THE DAY

(Serves 8)
Cheese Pastries with Pine Nut Salad
John Dory Baked with Asparagus
Piped Potatoes
Milleens Cheese
Gooseberry Fool

Wines

Fumé Blanc (California)
Cabernet Sauvignon (California)

The summery flavours of John Dory garnished with asparagus are greatly enhanced by the rich fruit of Fumé Blanc, which is also the choice to accompany the crunchy pastries. A Cabernet Sauvignon is the perfect partner for Milleens, a tangy farmhouse cheese. Gooseberry fool has a lovely pure fruit taste and looks very pretty in small glasses decorated with rose petals.

Timetable

The day before	Prepare the cheese pastries. Wash and chill the salad. Make the dressing. Prepare the potatoes. Make the gooseberry purée.
In the morning	Trim the fish. Prepare the asparagus. Finish the fool. Make the rose petal garnish.
1 hour before	Make the sauce for the fish and keep warm.
15 minutes before	Bake the cheese pastries. Arrange the salad. Put the fish and potatoes in the oven. Remove the fish just before starting the meal.
Before the main course	Reheat the fish quickly in a hot oven (200°C/gas 6) for two minutes.

Cheese pastries with pine nut salad

Prepare and bake the pastries

12 oz (350 g) goats"
cheese, preferably
cylindrical in shape
4 sheets filo pastry
1–2 oz (25–50 g)
melted butter
black pepper
1 tblsp virgin olive oil
4 sun-dried tomatoes,
cut in two

Remove the rind from the cheese and cut it into eight
portions, about 1–1½ inches (3–4 cm) in diameter
and half an inch (2 cm) thick; you may have to adapt
the exact size and shape to the type of cheese you are
using, but try to make neat, uniform pieces.
Brush two sheets of filo pastry with the melted butter
and lay the other two sheets on top.
Cut each double sheet into four.
Place a piece of cheese in the centre of each piece of
pastry, season with pepper and a few drops of olive oil
and top with half a sun-dried tomato.
Wrap the pastry around the filling in a neat, tight
parcel, trimming as necessary.
Chill until ready to bake.
Bake at 200°C/gas 6 for 12–15 minutes.

Prepare the salad and dressing

1 oak leaf lettuce
1 butterhead lettuce
1 punnet mâché or
lambs' lettuce
1½ tblsp wine vinegar
salt, black pepper
6 tblsp hazelnut oil
4 tblsp toasted pine nuts

Wash and dry the lettuces.
Tear the leaves into bite-sized pieces.
Chill until ready to serve.
Whisk together the vinegar and seasoning.
Whisk in the oil.
Toss the salad and pine nuts with the dressing.

To serve

Place an individual portion of salad on each plate.
Top with a hot pastry parcel and serve at once.

John Dory baked with asparagus

Prepare the fish and asparagus

16 fillets of John Dory
½ oz (12 g) butter
2 shallots
10 spears asparagus
1 pint (500 ml) water
3 tblsp white wine

Butter a gratin dish and sprinkle with the finely chopped shallots.
Skin the fish and lay it on top of the shallots. Chill until ready to cook.
Bring the water to the boil.
Trim the woody ends from the asparagus, slice into 2 inch (5 cm) pieces, and cook quickly in the boiling water until tender.
Drain, reserving four tablespoons of the cooking juices for the sauce.
Pour the wine over the fish and bake at 190°C/gas 5 for 10–12 minutes. (You can do this just before serving the first course.)
About five minutes before it is ready, add the asparagus to the fish to heat through.

Prepare the sauce

2 tblsp white wine vinegar
4 tblsp asparagus water
3 tblsp white wine
8 oz (225 g) butter
2 tblsp fresh chopped tarragon
salt, black pepper
lemon juice (if needed)

Boil the vinegar, asparagus water and wine together until reduced to about 3 tablespoons.
Off the heat gradually whisk in the butter as you would for beurre blanc, taking the pan on and off the heat so that the butter softens and emulsifies with the liquid but does not melt.
Stir in the herbs and season, adding some lemon juice if needed.
Keep warm until ready to serve (*see page 11*).

To serve

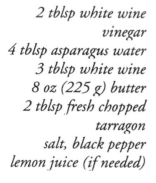
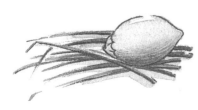

Serve two fillets of fish per person, topped with asparagus, with 2–3 tablespoons of the sauce, and a portion of piped potatoes.

Piped potatoes

2 lb (1 kg) floury potatoes (good varieties are Golden Wonder, Home Guard and King Edward)
2 oz (50 g) butter
2 eggs
salt, black pepper

Peel and boil the potatoes in salted water till cooked. Drain well.
Mash to a purée. Whisk in the butter and the beaten eggs. Season to taste.
Using a piping bag fitted with a star nozzle, pipe into eight portions in the shape of little towers.
When ready to serve the first course, bake the potatoes at 190°C/gas 5 for 15 minutes.

Milleens cheese

Milleens is made near Glengarriff on the West Cork/Kerry border from cows' milk. A soft, washed rind cheese, it gains in flavour and becomes creamier as it matures. Try to buy one that is ready to eat, as you are unlikely to be able to ripen it at home. Leave the cheese overnight in a cool place but never refrigerate. Serve Milleens with brown or walnut bread and perhaps a few walnuts in their shells.

Gooseberry fool

1¼ lb (600 g) gooseberries
4 oz (100 g) sugar
2 tblsp rosewater (available from pharmacies or Middle Eastern delicatessens)
2 oz (50 g) butter
10 fl oz (275 ml) cream
8 fine rose petals
1 egg white
6 tblsp caster sugar

Cook the gooseberries with the sugar until soft.
Crush to a purée, using a fork; you can use a blender if you wish, but a rough texture is also attractive.
Cool to lukewarm, then stir the rosewater into the purée. Whisk in the butter.
Cool completely, then fold in the whipped cream. Spoon the fool into individual glasses and chill.
Wash and dry the petals. Lightly fork the egg white. Dip the petals in the egg white, then into the sugar. Leave to dry.
Just before serving, decorate the glasses of fool with the petals.

WINES

First and second courses: Fumé Blanc (California)

Labels	Beringer, Napa Valley *or* Fetzer, Mendocino County *or* Mondavi, Napa Valley.
Availability	Widely available.
Drink	2 years old.
Serve	The wine should be chilled for a few hours in the fridge or for 8 minutes in ice and water. Open just before serving to maximise the aromas.
Taste	Fumé Blanc has an extremely attractive combination of flavours reminiscent of rhubarb and cream. It has citrus-type acidity with a waxy consistency and long, lingering flavours.
Awareness	California wine makers name their wines after the grape variety from which they are produced. 'Fumé Blanc' is the American term for sauvignon blanc. However, these wines rarely resemble sauvignon blanc wines from France. Less herbaceous, they are riper and fruitier in style, the best coming from the Napa and Sonomo Valleys.
Options	Glen Ellen from the Sonomo Valley. A good value Sauvignon Blanc is also available from Ernest and Julio Gallo.

Cheese course: Cabernet Sauvignon (California)

Labels	Mondavi Oakville, Napa Valley *or* Clos du Bois, Alexander Valley
Availability	Specialist wine shops.
Drink	5 years old.
Serve	Open two hours before serving at room temperature.
Taste	Enjoy the deep colour of these wines and their rich, oaky aromas. Overladen with warm spice-like cinnamon, the wines have a good bite of tannin which leaves a drying feeling in the mouth.
Awareness	Cabernet Sauvignon from the top Californian

producers are full-bodied tannic wines requiring time to mature. With their toasty oak influence, these are among the greatest red wines of California. The most famous are often compared with classed growths (crus classés) of Bordeaux.

Options   Widely available and offering good value for money are the softer Cabernet Sauvignon wines from Fetzer, Mondavi's Woodbridge and Ernest and Julio Gallo.

LATIN AMERICAN BUFFET

(Serves 12)
Chilled Avocado Soup
Chicken with Peppers and Chorizo
Mixed Bean Salad
Orange Rice
Crème Caramel and Summer Fruits

Wines

Fino Sherry (Spain)
Rioja Reserva (Spain)

A light cold *fino* sherry goes beautifully with the chilled starter of rich avocado soup. The main dish is a hearty casserole of chicken and pork with wine, herbs and peppers and chunks of spicy chorizo sausage. It is accompanied by a good Rioja, whose sweet, spicy fruit and dry vanilla oak bring out the flavours of the food while stimulating the appetite with its dry bite. The meal ends with a delicately flavoured crème caramel, served with summer fruits.

Timetable

Two days before	Make the chicken stock (*see page 6*).
	Cook the beans.
	Cook the chicken casserole.
The day before	Cook the rice.
	Finish the bean salad.
	Make the crème caramel.
In the morning	Make the avocado soup.
1 hour before	Reheat the chicken casserole.
15 minutes before	Unmould the caramels.
	Reheat the rice.

Chilled avocado soup

6 ripe avocados	Peel, stone and chop the avocados.
juice of 1 lemon	Blend to a purée with the lemon juice, cream and
10 fl oz (275 ml) cream	yoghurt.
10 fl oz (275 ml) plain	Transfer the mixture to a large bowl.
yoghurt	Add the peeled, crushed garlic and the chicken stock.
2–3 cloves garlic	Season with salt, pepper and Tabasco.
4 pints (2.25 litres)	Add the sherry.
white chicken stock	Taste and adjust the seasoning, adding a little sugar if
salt, black pepper	needed.
½ tsp Tabasco sauce	Chill.
2 tblsp dry sherry	Serve on the day it is made.

Chicken with peppers and chorizo

2 x 3 lb (1.5 kg) chickens, jointed into 8 pieces each
salt, black pepper
1½ lb (700 g) pork fillet
6 tblsp virgin olive oil
4 oz (100 g) piece of pale streaky bacon
8 oz (225 g) chorizo sausage
4 red peppers
1 Spanish onion
1½ pints (850 ml) chicken stock
10 fl oz (275 ml) red wine
4 tblsp tomato purée
4 cloves garlic, peeled and finely sliced

Slice the pork into pieces half an inch (2 cm) thick.
Heat half the oil. Fry the seasoned chicken and pork
until browned and slightly crisp. Place in a casserole.
Cube the bacon. Add to the remaining oil and fry
until beginning to crisp. Add to the meats.
Cut the chorizo into chunks. Fry until lightly
coloured, adding more oil if necessary. Add to the
meats.
Core and seed the peppers and chop roughly.
Chop the onion into chunks. Fry the pepper and
onion in the remaining oil. Add to the meats.
Drain the excess oil from the frying pan, pour in
3 tablespoons of stock, boil up and stir vigorously.
Add to the meats with the remaining stock, wine and
tomato purée. Add the garlic. Season well, cover and
cook over a low heat for 30 minutes. Uncover and
cook for 15–20 minutes. If the sauce is too liquid,
remove the meats and vegetables and boil the sauce
rapidly for 5 minutes. Return the meats and
vegetables to the casserole. Cool.
Reheat at 180°C/gas 4 for 30–40 minutes.

Mixed bean salad

1 lb (450 g) mixed beans: kidney, blackeye, flageolet	Soak the beans overnight in cold water. Add more water if necessary and boil rapidly for 10 minutes, then steadily for 40–50 minutes or until tender. Drain and cool.
3 tblsp vinegar	
salt, black pepper	Combine the vinegar and seasoning.
12 tblsp virgin olive oil	Whisk in the oil.
2 red onions	Add the beans to the vinaigrette with the finely
4 tblsp parsley	chopped onions and parsley.

Orange rice

5 fl oz (150 ml) white wine	Put the wine, stock, orange zest and turmeric into a saucepan and bring to the boil.
2½ pints (1.4 litres) chicken stock	In a separate saucepan, melt the butter and cook the onion without browning.
zest of 4 tangerine-type oranges	Add the rice and stir gently for 3 minutes. Add most of the stock mixture, cover and boil for
1 tsp turmeric	15–18 minutes, adding more stock if needed.
4 oz (100 g) butter	Season the rice and divide half of it between two
1 onion, finely chopped	lightly buttered loaf tins.
1½ lb (700 g) long grain rice	Peel and segment the tangerines and divide between the rice dishes.
salt	Spoon over the remaining rice and press well down.
black pepper	When cold, cover with foil and leave until ready to
12–16 tangerines	reheat.
	Reheat at 180°C/gas 4 for 15 minutes.

Cook's tip: Bean salad starter

❝A mixed bean salad makes a simple and cheap starter with appealing colours and textures. Mix the beans while still warm with the vinaigrette and other flavourings. Serve them on a bed of lettuce topped with little pieces of crisped bacon.❞

Crème caramel and summer fruits

·Make the crème

24 fl oz (70 ml) milk
10 fl oz (275 ml) cream
2 vanilla pods
8 eggs
6 oz (150 g) granulated sugar

Heat the oven to 160°C/gas 3.
Place the milk, cream and vanilla pods in a saucepan and bring to the boil.
Meanwhile, whisk the eggs and sugar.
Pour the boiling mixture on to the eggs and mix.
Pass through a sieve. Reserve.

Make the caramel

8 oz (225 g) granulated sugar
8 tblsp water

Have ready two 1½ pint (1 litre) deep dishes or moulds. Place the sugar and water for the caramel in a heavy saucepan and heat to dissolve the sugar. Bring to the boil and cook rapidly, without stirring, to a deep caramel. Pour into the moulds and swirl to coat the edges to a depth of about 1 inch (2 cm).

Bake the crèmes

Pour the crème into the moulds.
Cover the tops with tinfoil and stand in roasting tins.
Pour in cold water to a depth of about 1 inch (2 cm), transfer to the oven and bake for 35–40 minutes.
To test if the crème is set, uncover the mould and make a small cut in the centre of the custard with the point of a knife. If it is cooked, the cut mark will remain visible; if the edges run together again, return to the oven for a few more minutes.
Remove the caramels from the roasting tins.
Cool, then chill.

To serve

Turn out on to dishes with raised edges to hold the caramel. Serve with raspberries or strawberries.

– 107 –

WEEKEND BRUNCH

(Serves 12)
Kedgeree
Baked Gammon
Stuffed Mushrooms
Breakfast Sausages
Dried Fruit Compote
Yoghurt Bowl
Breakfast Ring Cake

Wines

Cava (Spain)
Riesling (Germany)

The relaxed mood starts with a glass or two of bubbly, delicious Cava from Spain. Kedgeree is a subtle blend of Indian and English cookery. Serve it as the star dish flanked by the best sausages you can find, flavoursome stuffed mushrooms and gammon baked with an old-fashioned breadcrumb crust. Keep the Cava flowing, but serve a fruity Riesling along with it for those who prefer a still wine. Yoghurt and fruit, eaten at any stage of the meal, add a light note to the menu. Finish with rich, almond-filled cake, piping hot coffee and a selection of Indian, China and herbal teas.

Timetable

The day before	Make the kedgeree.
	Sauté and fill the mushrooms.
	Make the fruit compote.
	Prepare and bake the breakfast ring.
	Cook and coat the bacon.
1 hour before	Prepare the yoghurt bowl.
	Cook the sausages. Bake the mushrooms.
	Reheat the kedgeree.

Kedgeree

6 oz (175 g) butter	Melt 2 oz (50 g) of the butter.
1 onion	Cook the finely chopped onion until it is transparent.
2 tsp mild curry paste	Stir in the curry paste and rice. Add the boiling water.
1 lb (450 g) long grain rice	Stir once, season, cover and boil for 15 minutes.
1¼ pints (575 ml) boiling water	Place the fish in a saucepan. Pour over the milk. Add enough water to cover. Cover, bring to the boil, remove from the heat and stand for 10 minutes.
salt, black pepper	Drain the fish, flake and mix into the rice. Chop the
2 lb (900 g) smoked haddock	hard-boiled eggs (roughly into eighths) and add to the rice. Season. Stir in the soured cream.
1 fl oz (25 ml) milk	Butter a deep oven dish and spoon in the kedgeree,
4 hard-boiled eggs	dot with the remaining butter and cover with foil.
5 fl oz (150 ml) soured cream	Refrigerate until ready to serve. Heat in the oven at 180°C/gas 4 for 30 minutes, stirring once.
2 tblsp watercress or parsley	Garnish with finely chopped watercress or parsley.

Baked gammon

Cook the gammon

3 lb (1.35 kg) corner gammon	Soak the gammon in cold water overnight. Drain. Rinse in cold running water. Place in a large sauce-
1 pint (550 ml) cider	pan. Add the cider and water to cover.
1 tblsp mustard powder	Bring to the boil. Add the mustard, sugar and pepper-
2 tblsp brown sugar	corns. Simmer for 1 hour. Cool in the water for 20
12 black peppercorns	minutes. Drain. Remove the skin and excess fat.

Make the crust and bake the gammon

4 oz breadcrumbs	Mix the stale breadcrumbs with the other ingredients
1 tsp mustard powder	for the crust and spread evenly over the fat.
1 tblsp brown sugar	Place the gammon in a roasting dish, pour in water to
zest of 1 orange	about half an inch (2 cm) depth. Bake at 190°C/gas 5
2 tblsp melted butter	for 40–45 minutes. Cool completely.

Stuffed mushrooms

30 medium, flat mushrooms	Clean the mushrooms and remove the stalks.
2 tblsp groundnut oil	Trim the woody ends from the stalks and discard.
salt	Chop the remainder finely.
black pepper	Heat the oil and cook the mushroom caps lightly.
4 oz (100 g) streaky rashers	Season and cool.
1 onion	Finely chop the bacon and onion and fry in half an ounce of butter with the mushroom stalks.
2 oz (50 g) butter	Finely chop the hard-boiled eggs.
2 hard-boiled eggs	Combine with the onion mixture and breadcrumbs.
6 oz (175 g) fresh bread-crumbs	Mix in the chopped thyme and season.
2 tblsp fresh thyme	Stir in the egg and milk.
1 egg whisked with 2 tblsp milk	Spoon the filling on to the mushroom caps and dot with the remaining butter.
	Bake at 180°C/gas 4 for 15 minutes.

Ingredients list (for clarity):

30 medium, flat mushrooms
2 tblsp groundnut oil
salt
black pepper
4 oz (100 g) streaky rashers
1 onion
2 oz (50 g) butter
2 hard-boiled eggs
6 oz (175 g) fresh bread-crumbs
2 tblsp fresh thyme
1 egg whisked with 2 tblsp milk

Cook's tip: Stuffed mushroom starter

❧*Stuffed mushrooms make a simple first course served with the following salad:*

1 butterhead lettuce	*Wash and dry the lettuces.*
1 bunch watercress	*Tear into bite-sized pieces.*
4 oz (100 g) redcurrants or blackberries	*Prepare the fruit.*
1 oak-leaf lettuce	*Add the fruit to the lettuces.*
2 tblsp raspberry vinegar	*Mix the vinegar with the mustard and seasoning.*
salt, black pepper	*Whisk in the oil.*
1 tsp Dijon mustard	*Stir in the mint.*
8 tblsp virgin olive oil	*To serve:*
1 tblsp chopped mint	*Allow 3–4 stuffed mushrooms per person. Place on a bed of dressed salad.*❧

Breakfast sausages

2 lb (900 g) pork sausages	Prick the sausages and arrange on a baking tray.
2 tblsp groundnut oil	Brush with oil.
	Bake for 20 minutes at 180°C/gas 4.

To serve

selection of mustards	Serve with a selection of mustards—Dijon, English and a sweet or honeyed mustard—and crusty bread.

Dried fruit compote

8 oz (225 g) dried prunes	Place the dried fruit in a large bowl.
8 oz (225 g) dried apricots	Cover with cold water and soak overnight.
	Place the fruit and the water in which it soaked in a saucepan.
8 oz (225 g) dried peaches	Add the sugar and simmer for 10 minutes.
4 tblsp brown sugar	Cool in the syrup.
2 oranges	Peel and segment the oranges and add to the fruit.

Yoghurt bowl

2 pints (1 litre) natural yoghurt	Place the yoghurt in a serving dish and chill.
3 oz (75 g) toasted flaked almonds	Just before serving, sprinkle over the almonds, chopped walnuts and chopped dates, then dribble the honey over the centre.
2 oz (50 g) walnuts	
4 oz (100 g) dates	
8 tblsp clear honey	

Breakfast ring cake

Make the dough

*12 oz (350 g) plain
flour
1 tsp baking powder
5 oz (150 g) butter
4 tblsp caster sugar
2 eggs
6 tblsp milk*

Sift the flour and baking powder.
Rub in the butter. Stir in the sugar.
Beat the eggs and milk and pour on to the flour.
Mix quickly to a light dough.
Turn on to a floured surface and roll into a rectangle about half an inch (2 cm) thick.
Fold the top third down and the bottom third up then turn through 90° and roll out again.
Repeat the rolling and folding twice more.
Roll out to a rectangle about 8 inches (20 cm) by 14 inches (35 cm).

Fill and bake the ring

*4 oz (100 g) fromage
frais
3 oz (75 g) ground
almonds
½ tsp vanilla essence
2 oz (50 g) caster sugar
3 oz (75 g) sultanas
1 egg, beaten
4 oz (100 g) icing sugar*

Mix the fromage frais, ground almonds, vanilla essence, caster sugar and sultanas and spread over the dough.
Roll up like a Swiss roll, then join the ends to make a ring.
Cut three-quarters of the way through the ring at 1 inch (2 cm) intervals all the way around.
Brush with the beaten egg.
Bake at 200°C/gas 6 for 20–25 minutes. Cool.
Mix the icing sugar with 1–2 tablespoons of cold water and dribble over the baked ring.

WINES

Throughout the meal: Cava (Spain)

Labels — Cordon Negro Freixenet.

Availability — Widely available.

Drink — 4 years old.

Serve — Chilled.

Taste — Cava has a fine quality mousse and an attractive straw colour. The nose is reminiscent of freshly baked bread and lightly toasted nuts. The flavour broadens out on the palate and the crisp acidity leaves a clean finish. The bead (or bubble) should be long and persistent.

Awareness — Cava is the name given to quality sparkling wines of Spain. The wine is made from traditional grapes such as macabeo, parellada and xarel-O. Some wine makers now add chardonnay to the blend. The sparkle is achieved by the traditional method of adding yeast and sugar to the still wine after the first fermentation. The wine is then bottled and sealed, which provokes a secondary fermentation in bottle. The gas cannot escape, dissolves in the wine and creates the bubble.

Options — Codorníu Premier Cuvée Brut non-vintage.

Throughout the meal: Riesling (Germany)

Labels — From the Deinhard Heritage range of village wines Johannisberg *or* Bernkastel.

Availability — Specialist outlets.

Drink — 6 years old.

Serve — Cool. Place in the fridge door for an hour.

Taste — Star bright with hints of green, the wine has delicate floral fruit aromas. Its fruity style with clean, limey acidity is reminiscent of a fresh green apple. Its lightness makes it ideal for brunch.

Awareness — The riesling grape produces Germany's finest wines, ranging in flavour from apple to rich honey dessert wines. Not cheap, but worth the money.

Middle Eastern salad

SUMMER BUFFET

(Serves 12)
Smoked Trout Mousse
Turkish Lamb and Bean Casserole
Bulghar Pilaff
Middle Eastern Salad
Summer Pudding
Wines
Vinho Verde (Portugal)
Minervois (France)

This is a simple yet deliciously different meal for a number of guests. The light fish starter is well partnered by the refreshing acidity and spritz of Vinho Verde while the aromatic casserole is complemented by oak-matured red Minervois. Bulghar pilaff is a nutty alternative to rice and the salad keeps the Mediterranean mood with its herbs and feta cheese. Traditional summer pudding ends the meal on a high note.

Timetable

The day before	Make the smoked trout mousse.
	Cook the lamb casserole.
	Make the summer pudding.
	Wash and chill the salad.
	Make the salad dressing.
In the morning	Make the pilaff.
1 hour before	Arrange the mousse for serving.
	Heat the casserole.
	Unmould the pudding.
	Heat the pilaff (for 15 minutes only).

Smoked trout mousse

1½ lb (700 g) smoked trout
6 oz (175 g) unsalted butter
6 oz (175 g) fromage frais
6 tblsp cream
2 tsp grated horseradish
salt
black pepper

Remove all skin and bones from the fish.
Mince finely in a food processor, or mash with a fork.
Add the butter and blend until smooth.
Add the fromage frais, cream, horseradish and seasonings to make a soft consistency.
Chill in a serving dish or individual ramekins.

To serve

Serve the mousse in ramekins or, for simplicity at a buffet, spread on to thin slices of lightly buttered brown bread and hand around on trays.

Cook's tip: Smoked mackerel

For a more economical but still delicious smoked fish mousse substitute smoked mackerel for the trout. In place of the horseradish, add 1–2 cloves of crushed garlic and the juice of one lemon.

Shopping tip: Bulghar

Bulghar is a cracked wheat grain which is popular in Middle Eastern countries for salads and pilaffs. It is highly nutritious and easy to prepare. You will find it in many supermarkets, continental delicatessen stores and health food shops. Serve smaller quantities than you would of rice—bulghar is extremely filling.

Turkish lamb and bean casserole

1½ lb (700 g) French beans
1 tblsp salt
5 lb (2.5 kg) boned shoulder lamb
salt
black pepper
4–6 tblsp flour
olive oil for frying
3 medium onions
4 cloves garlic
1½ tblsp cumin
8 fl oz (225 ml) red wine
1 lb (500 g) fresh tomatoes
1 can chopped tomatoes

Top and tail the beans and cut into strips.
Mix with the salt.
Place in a colander to drain for 1 hour.
Cut the meat into cubes, removing as much fat as possible and any sinew. (This is a fiddly job but it is essential to trim the meat thoroughly.)
Season the cubes of meat and roll in flour.
Heat the oil and brown the meat in batches until evenly coloured. Reserve.
Add the roughly chopped onions and garlic to the pan and cook until soft. Stir in the cumin.
Add the wine, the canned tomatoes, the peeled and chopped fresh tomatoes, meat and drained (but not rinsed) beans.
Bring to simmering point, cover and cook on the hob, at gentle simmer point, or in the oven at 140°C/gas 3, for 1½–2 hours.
If you have made the casserole in advance, gently reheat it in the oven for about 15 minutes, or on top of the stove. Be careful not to overcook it.

Bulghar pilaff

1¼ pints (500 ml) water
½ tsp salt
12 oz (350 g) bulghar
3 tblsp fresh mint
4 oz (100 g) raisins
12 spring onions
6 tblsp virgin olive oil
salt, black pepper

Bring the water to the boil, add the salt and bulghar, cover and cook for 10 minutes.
Remove from the heat, add the chopped mint, raisins and chopped spring onions.
Cover and keep warm in a low oven for 10 minutes. (This dish can be made up to a day in advance and then reheated in a warm oven for about 15 minutes.)
Just before serving stir in the olive oil and season to taste.

Middle Eastern salad

Prepare the salad

1 cos lettuce
8 large ripe tomatoes
4 red peppers
1 lb (450 g) feta cheese
3 oz (75 g) black
olives, stoned

Wash and dry the lettuce and tear into bite-sized pieces. Chill.
Arrange on a dish or in a salad bowl.
Cut the tomatoes into wedges.
Core and slice the peppers. Cube the cheese.
Add the peppers, tomatoes, olives and cheese.

Make the dressing

3 tblsp red wine vinegar
salt, black pepper
1 tsp dried oregano
12 tblsp virgin olive oil

Mix the vinegar, salt, pepper and oregano.
Whisk in the oil.
Just before serving, pour the dressing over the salad.

Summer pudding

4–6 oz (100–150 g)
granulated sugar
5 fl oz (150 ml) water
2½ lb (1.5 kg) mixed
red berries(e.g.
raspberries, strawberries,
redcurrants etc)
about 20 large slices
of good white bread
cream

Boil the water and sugar, stirring to dissolve the sugar.
Add the prepared fruit to the syrup.
Simmer for 5 minutes. Cool.
Drain the fruit, reserving the syrup.
Sprinkle two 1½ pint (650 ml) pudding bowls with water.
Trim the crusts from the bread. Starting with the base, line the bowls with the bread, leaving no gaps.
Spoon the drained fruit into the bread-lined bowls.
Cover the tops with more bread.
Fit plates over the tops and weigh down.
Chill overnight.

To serve

Turn the puddings out on to large plates. Spoon over the reserved syrup and decorate with the reserved fruit. Serve very cold with cream.

WINES

First course: Vinho Verde DOC (Portugal)

Labels	Aveleda Vinho Verde
Availability	Widely available.
Drink	1 year old.
Serve	As the appeal of this wine is its freshness of flavour and attractive spritz, serve it chilled straight from the wine cooler or fridge. Open the wine at the exact moment you are serving.
Taste	The wine should be pale with hints of green. Notice the hint of prickle and the way it dances agreeably around the mouth. It refreshes without hindering the mild fruit flavours and off dry finish.
Awareness	Vinho Verde means 'green wine', which is not a reference to colour but rather to the fact that the wine should be drunk very young in order to retain its freshness. It is produced from a blend of grape varieties including Azal Branco, Alvarinho and Loureiro, in the Minho district in northern Portugal. Here, there are many growers who own small plots of land. The grape is trained high in order to allow the cultivation of other fruits and vegetables underneath the vine.
Options	Good value Trajadura also from the Aveleda Estate

Main course: Minervois AOC (France)

Labels	Domaine Saint Germain *or* Château de Paraza, Chene Neuf.
Availability	Widely available; good value.
Drink	3 years old.
Serve	Open one hour before serving at room temperature.
Taste	The wine has scents of concentrated wild red berry fruits with hints of pepper and spice. There is also a trace of vanilla, the wine having been matured in oak.
Awareness	Minervois is a wine region in the Languedoc-

Roussillon region of southern France. Its wines are named after the ancient city of Minerva, a Roman stronghold dedicated to the goddess Minerva. Grape varieties include grenache, carignan and cinsault. The wine makers are working for official recognition of an established 'cru' system. A number of wine makers are experimenting with oak, which adds subtle tones to these rustic, herby wines.

Options Château Mirausse *or*, if you prefer a fruitier style, try Domaine Maris.

SUPPER IN THE KITCHEN

(Serves 8)
Risotto of Sun-dried Tomatoes
Veal Baked with Rosemary
Green Salad
Gruyère Cheese
Blackcurrant Bavarois
Wines
Gewurztraminer, Alsace (France)
Valpolicella (Italy)

Risotto is a wonderful dish, but it cannot be cooked in advance and must be served as soon as it is ready. You can only make this kind of dish when you can cook and chat, glass in hand, as guests appreciate the aromas of the food to come. The rich, spicy taste of sun-dried tomatoes and basil in this risotto goes beautifully with the Gewurztraminer. The main dish of thick veal cutlets baked in wine and herbs needs only a green salad and the rich, smooth flavour of a good Valpolicella. Both wines are good partners for the Gruyère cheese. The rich taste of the blackcurrant bavarois needs no accompaniment.

Timetable

The day before	Make the bavarois. Make the stock.
	Wash the salad and make the dressing.
1 hour before	Prepare the veal.
	Unmould the bavarois, decorate and refrigerate.
45 minutes before	Brown the veal.
30 minutes before	Start the risotto.
10 minutes before	Put the veal into the oven. Turn the cutlets over just before sitting down to the first course.

Risotto of sun-dried tomatoes

1¼ pints (750 ml) chicken stock (see page 6)
1 onion
2 cloves garlic
6 sun-dried tomatoes
1½ oz (35 g) butter
1 lb (450 g) arborio rice
4 fl oz (110 ml) white wine
bunch of basil, about 20 leaves
salt, black pepper
6 tblsp grated Parmesan cheese

Heat the stock to boiling point.
Finely chop the onions and garlic.
Roughly chop the sun-dried tomatoes.
Cook the onion, garlic and tomatoes gently in the butter until the onion is soft but not coloured.
Stir in the rice and cook for a minute or so.
Add the wine and a ladleful of hot stock.
Cook, stirring frequently, until the stock has been absorbed, then add another ladleful of stock and continue to cook, stirring all the time, until all the stock has been gradually added and the rice is tender but moist. It should move easily in the pan but not be mushy.
Season. Stir in the torn basil leaves and Parmesan cheese and serve at once.

Veal baked with rosemary

8 large veal cutlets (may need to be ordered)
salt
black pepper
3 tblsp olive oil
6 sprigs rosemary
3 cloves garlic
10 fl oz (275 ml) white wine

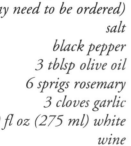

Trim and season the veal.
Note For this dish it is most important that the cutlets are properly prepared and trimmed before cooking.
Cut away all the chine bone—the 'T' part of the back remaining on the cutlet—or ask your butcher to do it for you.
Heat the oil and brown the cutlets over a high heat.
Place in a gratin dish and add the rosemary, the peeled and lightly crushed garlic and the wine.
Bake at 190°C/gas 5 for 20 minutes, turning once.

To serve

Serve the cutlets straight from the gratin dish with some of the herbs and cooking juices spooned over them.

Green salad

2 punnets mâché or
lambs' lettuce
1 tsp wine vinegar
juice of ½ lemon
1 tsp Dijon mustard
8 tblsp virgin olive oil
salt
black pepper

Separate and clean the salad leaves and arrange in a bowl.
Mix the vinegar, lemon and mustard.
Season and whisk in the oil.

To serve

Just before serving, toss the salad with the dressing.

Gruyère cheese

Gruyère cheese is mostly treated as a cooking cheese for sauces, soufflés and gratins. It generally only appears on the cheeseboard in the form of its close cousin, Beaufort. However, Gruyère is a delicious cheese with a sweet-sharp, slightly nutty flavour, which is good to eat on its own. Serve a big piece with some walnuts and warm, crusty French bread and sweet butter.

Shopping tip: Olive oil

❝The first pressing of olives produces the best quality oil—indicated on cans and bottles by the words 'virgin' or 'extra virgin'. Subsequent pressings, with greater pressure exerted, produce progressively cruder oil. 'Cold pressed' indicates that the oil was extracted without heat. Heat is used for lesser grades of oil and for commercial-scale production. Cold pressed, virgin olive oil from any of the Mediterranean countries gives the best and richest flavours, with subtle differences depending on the region. This is the oil to use for salads and special sauces. For general cooking and for blending with your finest oil, look for normal olive oil. The taste is lighter, so it is suitable for more varied use as well as being more economical.❞

Blackcurrant bavarois

12 oz (350 g)
blackcurrants
4–6 oz (100–150 g)
granulated sugar
¾ oz (20 g) gelatine
3 egg whites
6 oz (175 g) icing sugar
12 fl oz (350 ml) cream

Cook the blackcurrants with the granulated sugar.
Blend in a blender or food processor.
Rub the mixture through a sieve to remove the seeds.
Put 6 tablespoons of cold water in a cup or ramekin, sprinkle the gelatine over and leave for 5 minutes.
Heat gently (to warm, not hot) over hot water, to dissolve.
Stir into the blackcurrant purée.
Whisk the egg whites until stiff, then whisk in the icing sugar to make a glossy meringue.
Whisk the cream until it holds its shape.
Fold the meringue and cream into the blackcurrant purée.
Pour into one large mould or eight individual moulds or ramekins and put in the fridge to set.

To serve

If you have made a large bavarois, unmould it on to a serving dish by dipping the mould into hot water for 20–30 seconds and inverting on to a plate.
Decorate with cream and mint leaves and return to the fridge until serving.
Individual dishes can be served in ramekins or unmoulded on to plates.

Cook's tip: Gelatine

Gelatine comes in two forms, leaf and powdered. Leaf gelatine needs to be soaked before being added to the hot liquid. Powdered gelatine is also soaked in cold water then heated very gently to melt it. It should never get so hot that you cannot hold the dish in which it is heated. A microwave set on defrost is a good way to melt it, or stand the bowl containing the gelatine in hot water.
1 ounce of powdered gelatine = 6 leaves of gelatine

First course: Gewurztraminer AOC, Alsace (France)

Labels	F. E. Trimbach *or* Hugel et Fils.
Availability	Widely available.
Drink	2 years old.
Serve	Very cool. Place in the fridge for two hours.
Taste	Highly aromatic and extremely fat and 'oily' in the glass. The wine has aromas of rose petals, Turkish Delight and lychee fruit that follow through to the taste. The wonderful fruit flavours broaden out in your mouth and linger in a spicy finish.
Awareness	Gewurztraminer is said to be one of the easiest grapes to recognise when tasted blind. Its lowish acidity, high alcohol and scent of roses make it easily recognisable. The skins have a naturally deep colour, imparting deep golden tones to the wine. It is an extremely important grape variety in Alsace, where its style can range from dry and aromatic to rich and opulent. Easy to recognise by its perfume and hard to pronounce, it is worth trying with spicy food.
Option	Wolfberger.

Main course and cheese course: Valpolicella DOC (Italy)

Labels	Valpolicella Classico Superiore, Masi *or* Valpolicella Classico, Lamberti.
Availability	Widely available.
Drink	2 years old.
Serve	Open up to 1 hour before serving at room temperature.
Taste	Delightful garnet colours greet the eye. Cherry aromas are followed by delicious ripe fruit flavours. The long finish has an attractive bitter twist.
Awareness	Produced from the molinara, corvina and rondinella grapes, there are basically three different styles of

Valpolicella. Simple straightforward Valpolicella is all about up-front fruit flavours made for drinking young. At the opposite end of the spectrum are some of Italy's most individual and great red wines. Recioto and Amarone styles are produced from grapes picked about a week earlier than those of basic Valpolicella and laid on mats to dry. The grapes are left to shrivel, during which time the sugar increases, giving the base for wines that are rich in both flavour and alcohol. Fermentation then proceeds until the wine has reached 13–14 per cent with a certain amount of residual sugar (to become Recioto), or until the wine is fully dry (Amarone) at 15–16 per cent. Great complex wines with gamey mossy flavours and bittersweet fruit, the wines have a rich texture. In the third style of Valpolicella, Ripasso, the young wine is re-fermented on the lees (sediment) of the Recioto or Amarone, giving a fuller, richer wine. Masi's Campo Fiorin is a famous example.

Options   Bolla *or* the more expensive but highly recommended Masi single estate Serego Aligheri.

AUTUMN DINNER PARTY

(Serves 8)
Scallops with Leek Noodles
Pheasant with Horseradish Sauce
Artichoke Purée
Walnut Salad
St Nectaire Cheese
Clafoutis of Plums
Wines
Orvieto Classico (Italy)
Grand Cru Bourgeois (France)

Here is a meal using the best of autumn fare—pheasant, shellfish, young leeks, dark juicy plums and St Nectaire cheese. The delicate taste of glazed scallops is complemented by the bracing acidity of Orvieto. Grand Cru Bourgeois combines well with pheasant and matches the spice of the horseradish. The rich cheese with the Orvieto is followed by a plum clafoutis made with a sweet vanilla custard.

Timetable

The day before	Make the stock. Make the horseradish sauce.
	Make the artichoke purée. Wash and chill the salad.
	Make the pastry case and the custard for the clafoutis.
In the morning	Make the dressing. Cut and blanch the leeks.
2 hours before	Make the beurre blanc.
	Brown the pheasant.
30 minutes before	Bake the pheasant. Cook the scallops.
	Reheat the vegetables. Make the clafoutis.
5 minutes before	Reheat the horseradish sauce. Warm the leeks.

Scallops with leek noodles

6–8 young leeks
salt
8–16 scallops (depending on size)
black pepper
beurre blanc, made with
8 oz (225 g) butter
(see p.11)

Clean the leeks.
Cut into strips lengthways.
Bring some water to the boil and add salt.
Add the leeks and cook for 1 minute.
Pour the leeks into a colander and run cold water over them.
Make the beurre blanc and keep warm.
Cut each scallop into 2 or 3 horizontal slices.
Season with salt and pepper.
Cook in a non-stick pan for 30–40 seconds on each side until lightly coloured.
Before serving, warm the leeks gently.
Place the scallops on an oven tray and reheat for 1–2 minutes in a hot oven—180°C/gas 4.

To serve

Arrange some leeks in a 'nest' in the middle of each plate.
Place the scallop slices on top and pour over the sauce.

Pheasant with horseradish sauce

Prepare the pheasant breasts

4 pheasants

Cut the legs from the pheasants.
Reserve for another use.
Remove the breasts from the bone and reserve.
Cut up the carcasses and make stock (*see page 9*).

Make the sauce

1 shallot
1 oz (25 g) butter
5 fl oz (150 ml) white wine
10 fl oz (275 ml) pheasant stock
8 fl oz (225 ml) cream
1 tblsp grated horseradish

Sauté the finely chopped shallot in half an ounce of the butter.
Add the wine and stock and reduce to one-third.
Add the cream, season and simmer for 3 minutes.
Stir in the horseradish.
Season to taste.
Just before serving, whisk in the remaining butter.

Make the garnish

8 oz (225 g) shitake mushrooms
1 oz (25 g) butter

Wash and dry the mushrooms.
Slice the mushrooms and cook quickly in butter.
Reserve.

Cook the pheasant breasts

8 boned pheasant breasts
salt
black pepper
2 tblsp groundnut oil

Season the breasts. Heat the oil. Brown the breasts in the hot oil.
Place on a baking tray, cover with foil.
Cook for 10 minutes at 190°C/gas 5.

To serve

Serve in slices, garnished with sauce and mushrooms.

Artichoke purée

2½ lb (1 kg) Jerusalem
artichokes
salt
1 oz (25 g) butter
3 fl oz (150 ml) cream
3 fl oz (75 ml) milk
black pepper

Peel the artichokes and cut into cubes.
Barely cover with water, add a little salt.
Bring to the boil and cook for about 10 minutes until tender.
Drain thoroughly.
Work to a purée, adding the butter and cream.
Season to taste.
If you make the purée the day before, don't add the cream and butter until you reheat it.

Walnut salad

Prepare the salad

1 cos lettuce
1 butterhead lettuce
2 bunches watercress
2 oz (50 g) walnuts
2 tblsp walnut oil

Wash the lettuces and the cress and dry.
Break into bite-sized pieces.
Put the halved walnuts in a bowl.
Pour over 2 tablespoons of walnut oil.

Make the dressing

2 tblsp wine vinegar
1 tsp Dijon mustard
salt
black pepper
2 tblsp groundnut oil
6 tblsp walnut oil

Mix the vinegar and mustard.
Season.
Whisk in the oils.

To serve

Toss the salad with the dressing.
Garnish with the drained walnuts.

St Nectaire cheese

This delicate, semi-soft, rinded French cheese is at its best made from unpasteurised milk, so it's worth the effort to get the genuine farmer's product. This is indicated directly on the label of the cheese, so there can be no doubt. When buying, look for a greyish- or orange-tinted rind and a supple texture beneath it. If the cheese is cut, see that there are not too many holes, which indicate bitterness. It should have a mild aroma of mould or 'earthiness'. Serve the cheese with plenty of crusty bread—one flavoured with seeds or nuts is particularly successful.

Clafoutis of plums

Make the pastry case

8 oz (225 g) pâte sucrée
flour for rolling

On a floured surface roll out the pastry.
Line a 9 inch (23 cm) metal flan tin with the pastry.
Prick the base with a fork.
Chill for at least 30 minutes.
Heat the oven to 200°C/gas 6. Bake the pastry case for 7–8 minutes. Remove and cool.

Make the custard

10 fl oz (275 ml) cream
2 medium eggs
1½ oz (35 g) flour
5 oz (150 g) caster sugar

Heat the cream to just below boiling.
Whisk the eggs, flour and sugar together.
Pour the hot cream on to the mixture.
Mix and leave to cool.

Make the clafoutis

1 lb (450 g) plums
icing sugar

Slice the plums and arrange in the pastry case. Pour the custard over, and bake at 190°C/gas 5 for 20–30 minutes until the custard is set and lightly golden.

To serve

Serve warm, dusted with icing sugar.

WINES

First course and cheese course: Orvieto Classico Secco DOC (Italy)

Labels	Lamberti *or* Antinori *or* Luigi Bigi.
Availability	Widely available.
Drink	2 years old.
Serve	Serve chilled to retain its crisp character.
Taste	Notice the pale colour. The wine has good aromas, suggesting almonds and herbs. On the palate it is bone dry with a crisp, clean sweep to the subtle fruit. There is also a surprising length to the fruit in the finish.
Awarenes	From Umbria, in the centre of Italy, Orvieto is called after the town of the same name. Produced principally from the trebbiano and grechetto grapes, it was traditionally a medium-sweet wine. Drier versions are now more widely available and have become more popular. 'Abbaccato' on the label indicates a medium-sweet style; 'secco' indicates a dry style.
Optionss	Cecchi *or* Ruffino.

Main course: Grand Cru Bourgeois (France)

Labels	Château Loudenne *or* Château Potensac.
Availability	Widely available.
Drink	4 years old.
Serve	If possible the wine should be left at room temperature for 24 hours before drinking. Open the wine at least two hours before drinking to give it time to release its full bouquet
Taste	In a cru bourgeois wine you find the tastes of classic claret, the well-worn terms of blackcurrant, cedar and cigar, at a moderate level of development. The taste changes as the wine ages and it is largely a matter of personal preference as to when it is best to drink. The younger wine has more obvious blackcurrant, vigour

and bite, which is immensely satisfying with strong food, while as it ages the vigour diminishes and the taste changes from predominantly fruit to a mixture of elements leading to adjectives such as smoky, cigar-like. The wine has greater complexity and delicacy at this stage.

Awareness The classed growth wines of Bordeaux are beyond most everyday drinking budgets. However, the claret lover should be aware of the quality red wines available at affordable prices, for instance the cru bourgeois wines of the Médoc appellation. Look for the phrase 'cru bourgeois' on the label.

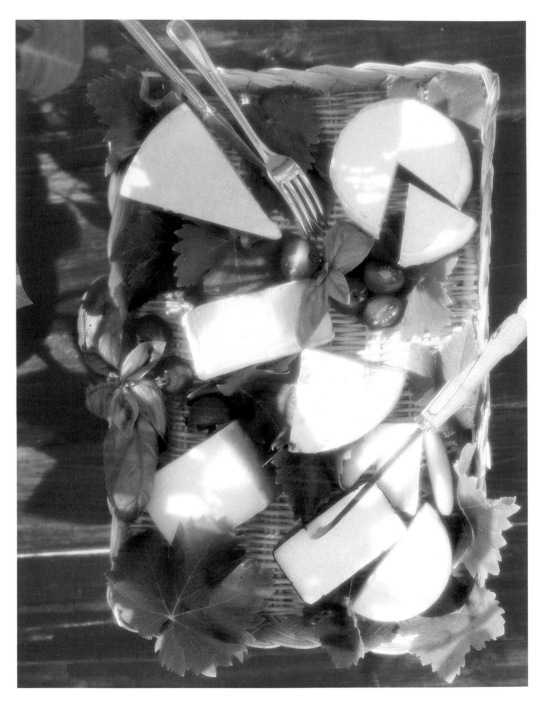

Irish Cheeseboard

OLD MEETS NEW

(Serves 8)
Salmon Terrine with Chive Mayonnaise
Rib of Beef with Grilled Marinated Vegetables
Aligot
Irish Cheeseboard
Fruit Strudel
Wines
Pinot Blanc, Alsace (France)
Shiraz (Australia)

Shiraz is one of the glories of Australian wine-making, This rich, gutsy red wine needs similarly flavoursome food and the rib of beef, with its colourful vegetables and garlicky aligot, is just the thing. The rich, creamy salmon terrine goes beautifully with the soft yet full flavours of the Pinot Blanc, and makes a subtle contrast to the robustness of the main dish. The spiciness of the Shiraz is wonderful combined with Cashel Blue, rich Cooleeney and rinded goats' cheese. The meal ends with a light strudel, a delicate, golden shell of filo pastry enclosing luscious summer fruits.

Timetable

The day before	Make the terrine and the mayonnaise.
	Prepare and marinate the vegetables.
In the morning	Add the herbs and cream to the mayonnaise.
	Make and chill the strudels.
2 hours before	Brown the beef.
	Make the aligot and keep warm.
	Grill the vegetables.
45 minutes before	Roast the beef. Bake the strudels.
	Reheat the vegetables.

Salmon terrine with chive mayonnaise

Make the mousse

9 oz (300 g) fresh raw salmon
1 egg white
10 fl oz (275 ml) cream
salt, black pepper
cayenne pepper

Place a bowl in the fridge to chill.
Mince the salmon finely in a food processor.
Blend in the egg white and work to a smooth purée.
Place in the chilled bowl.
Gradually stir in the cream.
Season to taste and chill.

Make the terrine

7 oz (200 g) fresh raw salmon
7 oz (200 g) sole
juice of 1 lime
3 tblsp chopped chives

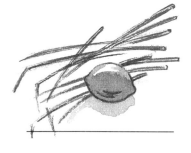

Cut the salmon and sole into strips.
Marinate in the lime juice for 30 minutes. Drain.
Line a terrine or loaf tin with non-stick paper. Spread one-third of the mousse in the terrine. Place a layer of fish strips over the mousse. Sprinkle with chives.
Layer again with one-third of the mousse, the remaining fish strips and chives.
Spread a final layer of mousse on top.
Cover the terrine with foil and stand in a roasting tin. Pour in cold water to come half-way up the sides of the terrine. Bake at 150°C/gas 3 for 1 hour.
Cool, then chill.

Make the chive mayonnaise

6 fl oz (150 ml) mayonnaise (see page 10)
6 tblsp whipped cream
2 tblsp chopped chives

Make the mayonnaise.
Fold the cream and chives into the mayonnaise.

To serve

Serve the terrine cut in slices with one tablespoon of mayonnaise per person.

Rib of beef with grilled marinated vegetables

Marinate the vegetables

1 large aubergine
2 courgettes
5 tblsp virgin olive oil
1 red pepper
1 green pepper
4 sun-dried tomatoes
1 tblsp basil
1 tblsp thyme
½ tblsp rosemary
2 cloves garlic

Heat the grill, grill-pan or barbecue until very hot.
Slice the aubergine and courgettes.
Grill until browned on each side, brushing with oil.
Grill the peppers until blackened. Cool.
Peel the peppers, remove the seeds, core and slice.
Combine the peppers, aubergine and courgettes.
Chop the sun-dried tomatoes.
Peel and finely chop the garlic.
Add the tomatoes and garlic to the vegetables with the herbs, remaining olive oil and seasoning.
Marinate for at least 30 minutes.
Reheat gently just before serving.

Cook the beef

3–4 lb (1.35–1.8 kg)
rib of beef
salt
black pepper
olive oil
6 tblsp white wine

Season the beef.
Heat a frying pan until very hot.
Add a little oil and brown the meat briskly on both sides.
Roast for 20 minutes at 190°C/gas 5.
Remove from the oven and leave to stand for 5 minutes.
Pour the wine into the roasting tin and boil up, stirring to incorporate the sediment and concentrate the juices.

To serve

Carve the meat in thin slices, dress with a spoonful of wine-flavoured juice and serve with the vegetables.

Aligot

2 lb (1 kg) floury potatoes	Peel and boil the potatoes until soft.
3 oz (75 g) butter	Mash to a purée.
8 fl oz (250 ml) cream	Add the butter, cream and enough milk to give a creamy smooth consistency.
8 fl oz (250 ml) milk	Over a low heat add the cheese and peeled, crushed garlic.
4 oz (100 g) grated Gruyère or Cheddar cheese	Season to taste.
2 cloves garlic	Keep warm until serving.
salt	
black pepper	

Irish cheeseboard

Cooleeney Camembert is a full-fat, chalk rind soft cheese, made in the same way as Camembert, but from the milk of a single farm. When fully ripe, which is the way to eat it, it is very rich and creamy in texture and strong and tangy in flavour. *Cashel Blue* is a well-flavoured blue cheese with plenty of characteristic sharpness of taste. It has a smooth texture and fine veining. Look for a well-dispersed mould with a creamy-white background. The pink shading in the rind is characteristic of the area and is not a fault. Cover the cut surface and store in a cool place but not in the fridge. *Croghan* is a rinded goats' cheese with a rich, distinctive flavour. It is very good as part of a cheese selection as its mild acidity gives a very clean taste which contrasts with the other cheeses. Serve this selection with some fresh brown and white bread, butter and perhaps a few green apples.

Cook's tip: Cream cheese filling

A mixture of cream and fromage frais instead of whipped cream is delicious with most summer fruits. Try serving a bowl of raspberries or strawberries or a combination with lightly sweetened fromage frais or cream cheese mixed half and half with whipped cream. The slightly acidic bite from the cheese greatly enhances the fruit.

Fruit strudel

8 oz (225 g) strawberries	Hull the strawberries and cut in half.
8 oz (225 g) raspberries	Mix with the raspberries.
6 oz (175 g) fromage	In another bowl, mix the fromage frais, caster sugar,
frais	ground almonds and orange zest.
3 oz (75 g) caster sugar	Melt the butter.
4 oz (100 g) ground	Take the sheets of filo pastry.
almonds	*Note* For a strudel it is easier to use large sheets. If you
zest of 1 orange	are using the smaller ones join them together with
4 large or 8 small sheets	melted butter to make larger sheets.
filo pastry	Place a sheet of filo pastry on the worktop, brush with
2–3 oz (50–75 g) butter	melted butter and sprinkle with breadcrumbs.
2 oz (50 g) dried	Lay another sheet on top, brush with more butter and
breadcrumbs	continue the layers until all the pastry is used up,
icing sugar for dusting	brushing the final sheet with butter.
	Spread the fromage frais and ground almond mixture
	over the pastry and sprinkle the fruit on top.
	Roll up like a loose Swiss roll.
	Bake at 200°C/gas 6 for 20–25 minutes.
	Sprinkle with icing sugar and serve warm.

WINES

First course: Pinot Blanc AOC Alsace (France)

Labels	'Cuvée les Amours', Hugel et Fils *or* Schlumberger.
Availability	Widely available.
Drink	2 years old.
Serve	Chilled. Open just before drinking.
Taste	A very pale wine with delicate, apple blossom aromas, Pinot Blanc has light fruit on the palate, backed up by steely acidity, leaving a crisp, clean finish.
Awareness	Pinot Blanc's easy drinking style makes it particularly good as an aperitif or with food. The grape is grown extensively in Alsace.

Options	Zind Humbrecht is hard to find but is worth the effort.

Main course: Shiraz (Australia)

Labels	Hardy's Eileen Hardy Reserve *or* Penfolds' Bin 128.
Availability	Widely available.
Drink	3 years old.
Serve	Open at least two hours before serving to allow the wine to breathe. Serve at room temperature.
Taste	The wine has a dense, sometimes almost inky colour, with shades of purple, especially when young. It also shows high viscosity in the glass. Aromas are reminiscent of plums and blackberries as well as peppery, minty qualities. The palate is filled with luscious fruit, drawn out into flavours of pepper and other spices and ending in a dry satisfying finish.
Awareness	The grape the French call syrah is called shiraz by the Australians. Vast amounts of red wine are produced in Australia from shiraz. Styles range from the most famous and complex Penfolds' Grange Hermitage to the juicy, jammy wines of over-cropped vines. Excellent rich full-bodied shiraz-based wines are produced in the Hunter Valley.
Options	Brown Brothers, Wolf Blass, Rothbury Estate and Mitchelton Estate are all excellent producers of shiraz-based wines.

DINNER
FOR
VEGETARIANS

(Serves 8)
Tomato and Basil Soup
Filo Pastries with Two Sauces
Mint Sorbet
Feta Cheese en Papillote
Green Salad, Wild Rice Pilaff
Chocolate Cake
Wines
Dry Rosé (France *or* Spain)
Periquita (Portugal)
Banyuls (France)

In this meal, a succession of courses provides plenty of contrasting tastes, textures and colours. A light tomato and basil soup, oven-cooked to bring out the flavour, is followed by spicy vegetable pastries served with sweet and tangy sauces. A refreshing mint sorbet leads into the main dish of feta cheese baked in a parcel, served with a pilaff of wild rice and green salad. A luscious chocolate cake is a satisfying end to the meal.

Timetable

The day before	Make the soup. Cook the pilaff.
	Make and freeze the sorbet. Make the cake.
	Prepare the pastries and sauces.
In the morning	Wash the salad. Make the dressing.
	Prepare the cheese papillotes. Fill the cake.
15 minutes before	Bake the pastries. Reheat the soup and pilaff.
	Remove the sorbet from the freezer.
	Bake the cheese papillotes.

Tomato and basil soup

3 lb (1.35 kg) ripe tomatoes	Roughly chop the tomatoes without removing the skins.
2–3 cloves garlic	In a heavy casserole combine the tomatoes with the
10 leaves basil	peeled, chopped garlic, torn basil, olive oil, seasoning,
2 tblsp extra virgin olive oil	sugar and water.
salt, black pepper	Cook in the oven at 160°C/gas 3 for 45 minutes.
1 tsp sugar	Remove and rub through a sieve.
10 fl oz (225 ml) water	Taste and adjust the seasoning.
3 tblsp pesto	When ready to serve, reheat the soup and garnish each portion with a teaspoon of pesto.

Filo pastries with two sauces

Make the yoghurt and cucumber sauce

10 fl oz (275 ml) plain yoghurt	Pour the yoghurt into a bowl and mix lightly.
3 inch (8 cm) piece cucumber	Peel and grate the cucumber.
1 clove garlic	Peel and finely chop the garlic.
juice of ½ lemon	Add the cucumber and garlic to the yoghurt with the lemon juice and seasoning.
salt, black pepper	Chill until ready to serve.

Make the carrot and apricot sauce

2 medium carrots	Peel and chop the carrots.
zest and juice of 1 orange	Place in a saucepan and cover with water, orange juice and zest and apricots.
4 oz (100 g) dried apricots	Cover and boil for 5–10 minutes until soft.
	Blend to a purée and chill until ready to serve.

2 lb (900 g) boiled
potatoes
4 tblsp groundnut oil
1 onion
1 fresh green chilli
1 inch (2.5 cm) piece
root ginger
3 tblsp parsley
6 oz (160 g) frozen peas
1 tsp ground cumin
1 tsp coriander
1 tsp garam masala
½ tsp cayenne pepper
salt
juice of 1 lemon
6 sheets filo pastry
3 oz (75 g) butter

Peel and dice the potatoes.
Heat the oil and fry the finely chopped onion until just beginning to brown.
Remove the seeds from the chilli and chop finely.
Chop the ginger and parsley finely.
Add to the onions with the chilli, peas and 4 tablespoons of water.
Cover and simmer for 5–10 minutes.
Add the potatoes, spices, salt and lemon juice. Cool.
Melt the butter. Brush a sheet of filo pastry with butter and cut into three strips.
Place a heaped teaspoonful of the filling at the top of each strip of pastry, fold in the sides and roll up.
Place on a baking tray and brush lightly with melted butter. Repeat until all the pastry and filling are used up. Chill until ready to bake.
Bake the pastries at 200°C/gas 6 for 15 minutes until golden and crisp.

To serve

Serve on individual plates with a tablespoonful of each sauce on either side.

Mint sorbet

12 oz (375 g) sugar
15 fl oz (425 ml) water
1 tblsp China tea
2 oz (50 g) mint leaves

Boil the sugar and water. Add the tea, leave to stand for 1 minute, then strain. Add the mint.
Cool completely, strain into a shallow container.
Place in the freezer for 45 minutes.
Remove and whisk vigorously. Return to the freezer and then whisk twice more until half frozen.
Whisk for the last time with an electric mixer or process until smooth.
Return to the freezer in a covered container.
Remove from the freezer 1 hour before serving.

Feta cheese en papillote

2 lb (900 g) Greek feta
cheese
2 tblsp chopped oregano
4 tblsp virgin olive oil
8 sun-dried tomatoes
black pepper

When you are buying the cheese have it cut into four square slices, about 1 inch (3 cm) thick.
Cut the cheese slices in half, to make eight squares.
Take eight pieces of greaseproof paper large enough to enclose completely the pieces of cheese.
Place a piece of cheese in the centre of each piece of paper.
Sprinkle with oregano and olive oil.
Top with a sun-dried tomato and season with pepper.
Fold over the paper and seal the edges very well (a bit like a Cornish pasty) so that no steam escapes.
Heat the oven to 190°C/gas 5.
Bake the papillotes for 8–10 minutes.

To serve

Serve the papillotes on individual plates. Delicious aromas emerge when the parcels are opened.

Cook's tip: Halumi cheese kebabs

❡If you can find Greek halumi cheese, a hard sheeps' cheese available from specialist shops, it too makes an excellent vegetarian main dish. You will need about 2 lb (900 g). Cut the cheese into 1 inch (2 cm) cubes. Marinate for two hours in four tablespoons of virgin olive oil with a teaspoon of oregano and a teaspoon of rosemary. Season with black pepper. Thread the cheese on to skewers and grill briskly under a hot grill for about 5 minutes, turning frequently and basting with the marinade.❡

Green salad with mustard dressing

1 butterhead lettuce	Wash the lettuces and spinach.
4 oz (100 g) young spinach leaves	Tear into bite-sized pieces.
	Finely chop the herbs and mix.
1 radicchio lettuce	Crush the peeled garlic.
2 tblsp parsley	Mix the garlic with the vinegar and mustard.
2 tblsp marjoram	Season.
2 tblsp chives	Whisk in the olive oil.
1 tsp rosemary	Just before serving toss the lettuces, spinach and herbs
1 tsp thyme	with the dressing.
2 cloves garlic	
2 tblsp Balsamic vinegar	
2 tsp Dijon mustard	
salt, black pepper	
8 tblsp virgin olive oil	

Wild rice pilaff

4 oz (100 g) wild rice	Rinse the rices thoroughly.
4 oz (100 g) brown long grain rice	Heat 2 tablespoons of oil and fry the onions until transparent.
3 tblsp groundnut oil	Add the rices and cook for a minute or two.
1 onion	Add 1½ pints (650 ml) of hot water, salt and pepper,
salt, black pepper	cover and cook for 40 minutes.
4 oz (100 g) mushrooms	Slice the mushrooms, heat the remaining oil, and
3 tblsp toasted pine nuts	cook.
	Add to the cooked rice with the pine nuts.

Serve the rice at once or cool and refrigerate until ready to serve.
Reheat at 180°C/gas 4 for 15 minutes.

Chocolate cake

Make the sponge

4 medium eggs
4 oz (100 g) caster sugar
4 oz (100 g) plain flour

Heat the oven to 180°C/gas 4. Take a 2 inch (5 cm) deep, 8 inch (20 cm) diameter cake tin and cover the base with greaseproof paper.
Whisk the eggs and sugar until thick and mousse-like.
Sieve the flour and fold in.
Pour into the prepared cake tin and bake for 25 minutes.
Remove from the oven and invert on to a tea towel.
Leave to cool and remove the tin.

Fill the cake

2 egg whites
6 oz (150 g) icing sugar
12 oz (375 g) plain chocolate
6 fl oz (160 ml) cream

Put the egg whites and 4 oz (100 g) icing sugar into a heatproof bowl. Whisk over hot water until warm.
Transfer to another bowl and whisk to a stiff, glossy meringue.
Melt 8 oz (225 g) chocolate in a bowl over hot water.
Whisk the cream until softly stiff.
Fold together the cream, meringue and chocolate.
Cut the cold cake into three layers.
Place one layer on a plate and spread with about a quarter of the filling.
Place another layer on top and spread with another quarter of the filling.
Place the third layer on top.
Spread the remaining filling over the whole cake, top and sides. Chill until ready to decorate and serve.

To decorate and serve

Grate the remaining piece of chocolate over the cake.
Sieve the remaining icing sugar over the centre.

WINES

First and second courses: Dry Rosé (France or Spain)

Labels	Listel-Gris, Gris de Gris (France) *or* De Casta Rosado, Torres (Spain).
Availability	Fairly available.
Drink	Very young—1 year old at most.
Serve	Chilled. Open just before serving and keep chilled after opening.
Taste	Rosé wines can vary in colour from light pink to orange to salmon. They are easy to drink wines with light fruity aromas and flavours.
Awareness	Rosé, rosato, rosado, blush are all names for a wide variety of 'pink' wines. They range in style from dry and medium to sweet and in colour from onion-skinned, orange and pink to salmon. Rosé wine is not a blend of red and white wine. Red wine gets its colour from the skins of red grapes that are left in contact with the fermenting must (the juice from pressed grapes). The most common method of achieving a rosé wine is to leave the fermenting wine in contact with the red grape skins for a short period.
Options	Torres Santa Digna, Rosado, from Chile.

Main course: Periquita (Portugal)

Labels	Periquita José Maria da Fonseca *or* Torres Vedras, João Santarem.
Availability	Fairly available.
Drink	4 years old.
Serve	Open 1 hour before serving at room temperature.
Taste	Dense ruby in colour with rich, concentrated prune/raspberry scents. The wine hits the palate with delicious ripe raspberry fruit flavours followed by supple tannins and a slightly austere twist that does not conceal the long flavoursome finish.

Awareness	Portugal produces a huge diversity of wines from its own native red and white grape varieties as well as the classic or noble varieties planted around the world such as cabernet sauvignon and chardonnay. Periquita (little parrot) is the name of one of the native Portuguese red grapes. It is one of the most widely planted grapes in southern Portugal and causes confusion as it is also known as João de Santarem and Castelão Frances.

Last course: Banyuls AOC (France)

Labels	Banyuls Rimage.
Availability	Specialist wine outlets.
Drink	5 years old.
Serve	Serve at room temperature. There is no need to open it in advance.
Taste	The wonderful dark garnet colour reveals aromas of raisins, plums and caramel. The wine has a smooth velvety texture, backed up with good alcohol levels. It has great length of flavour and a delicious, uncloying sweetness remains on the palate.
Awareness	'Vins doux naturels' is the term used to cover the fortified sweet dessert wines from the south of France. Grape spirit is added to stop fermentation at an early stage. This results in a naturally sweet wine with an alcohol content ranging from 15 to 21 per cent. White vins doux naturels are produced from the muscat grape, while dark or red ones are produced from the grenache. Banyuls is grenache-based and named after the area it comes from in Languedoc-Roussillon.
Option	Three-year-old Domaine de la Rectorie.

SUNDAY LUNCH

(Serves 8)
Avocado Salad
Bacon en Croûte with Tarragon Sauce
Spicy Potatoes
Stir-fried Vegetables
Camembert Cheese
Hazelnut Meringue Cake
Wines
Sauvignon Blanc (Chile)
Zinfandel (California)

The meal starts on a light note with a fresh-tasting salad of avocados and cheese enhanced by the pure fruit and crisp acidity of Sauvignon Blanc. This wine is also good as an aperitif. The abundance of fruit and spicy, oaky tastes of the Zinfandel give a wonderful extra flavour to the salty, smoky bacon, and make an excellent partner for ripe Camembert. The sweetness of the meringue is offset by the subtle flavour of the nuts and the rich chocolate filling.

Timetable

The day before	Cook the bacon, allow it to cool and wrap it in pastry.
	Make the meringue cake.
In the morning	Make the dressing.
	Prepare the salad (excluding the avocados).
	Make the tarragon sauce.
	Cook the potatoes. Prepare the vegetables.
30 minutes before	Arrange the salad. Bake the bacon.
	Sauté the potatoes and keep warm.
	Stir fry the vegetables and keep warm.
After the first course	Heat the sauce.

Avocado salad

Make the dressing

2 tblsp wine vinegar
1 tsp Dijon mustard
salt
black pepper
8 tblsp virgin olive oil

Mix the vinegar with the mustard, salt and pepper. Whisk in the oil.

Prepare the salad

12 cherry tomatoes
8 oz (225 g) fresh
mozzarella cheese
1 tblsp chives
2 tblsp basil
1 clove garlic
4 ripe avocados

Cut the tomatoes in half. Cube the mozzarella cheese. Peel the garlic.
Mix together the cheese and tomatoes, then sprinkle with the chopped chives, torn basil leaves and finely chopped garlic.
Just before serving, peel, stone and slice the avocados and add to the salad.

To serve

3 oz (75 g) whole
Parmesan cheese

Dress the salad and arrange a portion on each plate. Shave some Parmesan cheese over each portion.

Shopping tip: Avocados

❛It is difficult to judge the condition of avocados, so it's wise to buy more than you need. The smooth-skinned variety should be green in colour and slightly soft when you cradle them in your hand. The skins of the rough-skinned variety are a much darker colour when ripe, almost black, and do not yield to pressure. If your avocados are slightly under-ripe, wrap them in news-paper and leave overnight in a warm room. Do not refrigerate. Over-ripe avocados can sometimes be bought cheaply and can be used for dips and sauces.❜

Bacon en croûte with tarragon sauce

3 lb (1.35 kg) loin back bacon
8 oz (225 g) puff pastry
flour
1 egg, beaten

Trim the meat so that only the 'eye' with a single layer of fat remains.

Reserve the trimmings, which can be used for stuffings and sauces.

Place the bacon joint in a gratin dish and add water to a depth of half an inch (2 cm).

Cover with foil and bake at 180°C/gas 4 for 1 hour. Cool completely.

On a lightly floured surface roll out the pastry very thinly—one-eighth of an inch (4 mm).

Place the bacon in the centre of the pastry. Bring up the sides to enclose the bacon.

Seal the edges well with beaten egg.

Decorate with the remaining pastry and brush the parcel with beaten egg. Chill for at least 30 minutes.

Bake the bacon

Heat the oven to 200°C/gas 6. Bake the bacon for 30 minutes.

Remove and leave to rest for about 5 minutes.

Make the tarragon sauce

5 fl oz (150 ml) white wine
7 fl oz (200 ml) chicken stock
3 sprigs tarragon
2 tsp Dijon mustard
1 tblsp tomato paste
8 fl oz (225 ml) cream
salt, black pepper

Boil the wine, stock and tarragon until reduced to about one-third.

Add the mustard, tomato paste and cream. Simmer for 5 minutes.

Remove the tarragon sprigs.

Season to taste.

Spicy potatoes

3 lb (1.35 kg) tiny potatoes
3 oz (75 g) butter
2 shallots
2 tsp mild curry paste
salt

Boil or steam the potatoes until tender.
Heat the butter and cook the shallots until transparent.
Stir in the curry paste and cook for 1 minute.
Add the potatoes and cook, stirring all the time, until hot and well flavoured with the curry. Season with salt to taste.

Stir-fried vegetables

2 carrots
2 courgettes
1 red pepper
½ head celery
1 inch (2.5 cm) piece root ginger
1 clove garlic
2–3 tblsp sesame oil
2 tblsp sesame seeds

Peel the carrots and cut into matchsticks.
Cut the courgettes, pepper and celery into similar-sized pieces.
Finely chop the ginger and the garlic.
Heat the oil im a wok or large frying pan and add the ginger and garlic.
Add the prepared vegetables and quickly stir fry for about 3 minutes.

To serve

Place in a warmed serving dish. Sprinkle with the sesame seeds and serve immediately.

Camembert cheese

This great cheese of Normandy is always a good choice for the end of a meal as it has so many admirers. Two whole cheeses look well and are the right size for a lunch or dinner party. The French, and the Normans in particular, like Camembert under-ripe, while in Ireland most people prefer a creamy consistency. Buy it ready to eat, in the condition you like best. Keep the cheese in a cool place, not in the fridge, and serve whole with bread and biscuits.

Hazelnut meringue cake

Make the cake

4 oz (100 g) hazelnuts
3 oz (75 g) icing sugar
2 tblsp flour
5 egg whites
2 oz (50 g) caster sugar

Heat the oven to 180°C/gas 4. Put the hazelnuts on to a baking tray and roast for about 15 minutes until the skins crack.
Rub in a sieve or tea towel to remove the skins. Leave the nuts to cool completely.
Heat the oven to 140°C/gas 2.
Grind the nuts finely in a food processor, adding the icing sugar and flour.
Whisk the egg whites until stiff, then gradually whisk in the caster sugar.
Fold the nut/flour mixture into the meringue.
Place two sheets of non-stick baking paper on oven trays. Mark a 9 inch (23 cm) circle on each one and pipe or spread the meringue on to this.
Bake for 40 minutes. Cool.

Make the filling

6 oz (175 g) bitter chocolate
12 fl oz (350 ml) cream
2–3 tblsp icing sugar

Melt the chocolate. Whip the cream until softly stiff. Fold the melted chocolate into the cream, working carefully.
Place a meringue circle on a plate and spread with filling. Cover with the other meringue.
Dust the top with icing sugar.
Chill until ready to serve.

WINES

First course: Sauvignon Blanc (Chile)

Labels
Availability
Drink

Errazuriz *or* Carmen *or* Undurraga.
Widely available.
1 year old.

Serve	Chill for three hours in the fridge. To enjoy the freshness of this wine, open just before serving.
Taste	Bright and pale in colour with hints of green, the appeal of this wine lies in its ripe fruit aroma, reminiscent of gooseberries. The taste is cut through by the fresh acidity characteristic of the grape, but it is generally softer and riper than Loire sauvignon.
Awareness	The wines chosen for this menu come from the important Central Valley region, one of the regions in Chile producing quality wines. It includes the zones of Maipo, Curico, Rapel and Maule, which produce top-quality wines.
Options	Montes *or* Santa Rita Casa.

Main course: Zinfandel (California)

Labels	Beringer *or* Frog's Leap.
Availability	Reasonably widely distributed.
Drink	5 years old.
Serve	Open the wine at least an hour before serving at room temperature, or slightly below—about 16°C.
Taste	Enjoy the wonderful deep rich colour which rolls around the glass like oil as you swirl it. Swirling helps to release aromas of ripe blackberry fruits overladen with smoky oak. This is carried through on the palate with a hint of spice in the finish.
Awareness	All the classic red and white grape varieties are grown in the US. Zinfandel, a red grape variety, is native to California. It ranges in style from dry to sweet, and in colour can be white, blush (rosé) or red. Traditionally, zinfandel was used to make everyday drinking wine known in the US as jug wine. Serious wine makers are now beginning to realise the potential of zinfandel, producing complex wines with an ability to age.
Options	Fetzer, Stratford.

CHRISTMAS DINNER

(Serves 8)
Oysters with Spicy Sausages
Roast Stuffed Goose
Pan-fried Potatoes
Bread Sauce
Parsnip and Apple Purée
Glazed Beetroot
Gorgonzola Cheese
Christmas Pudding with Brandy Sauce
Wines
Champagne *brut* (France), Chablis (France)
Côte de Beaune Villages (France)
Muscat de Beaumes-de-Venise (France)

The contrasting tastes of the cold, rich oysters and the hot, spicy sausages are magically washed down by Champagne or Chablis. Côte de Beaune Villages lifts the rich goose and side dishes. The Muscat combines delightfully with the tangy bite of Gorgonzola and stands up well to the spice and fruit in the pudding.

Timetable

Three months before	Make the Christmas pudding.
The day before	Cook the beetroot.
	Peel and slice the potatoes and cover with cold water.
4 hours before	Make the stock, stuffing and parsnip purée.
	Stuff the goose and start the cooking.
2 hours before	Make the bread sauce.
30 minutes before	Cook the potatoes. Start to boil the pudding.
	Cook the sausages. Make the gravy. Open the oysters.
	Reheat the vegetables. Make the brandy sauce.

Oysters with spicy sausages

2 lb (900 g) spicy pork
sausages
4 dozen oysters (order in
advance)
4 lemons

Prick the sausages and place on a baking tray.
Cook at 200°C/gas 6 for 20 minutes.
Open the oysters and arrange on a platter or
individual plates.
Garnish with lemon wedges.

To serve

Hand around the oysters and the sausages (with sticks)
before sitting down to the main course.

Roast stuffed goose

Stuff the goose

6 oz (175 g) dried
prunes
4 oz (100 g) dried
apricots
10 lb (4.5 kg) goose
1 onion
1 clove garlic
8 oz (225 g) piece
of smoked bacon
2 oz (50 g) butter
3 oz (75 g) dried
breadcrumbs
2 oz (50 g) walnuts
2 tblsp chopped parsley
½ tblsp rosemary
1 egg
salt, black pepper

Soak the prunes in red wine overnight.
Soak the apricots in water overnight.
Remove the goose from the fridge a few hours before
cooking to let it come to room temperature.
Peel and finely chop the onion and garlic.
Cube the bacon.
Melt the butter and cook the onion for 5 minutes.
Add the garlic and bacon and cook gently for 10
minutes.
Drain the fruit, reserving the wine from the prunes
for the gravy.
Stone and chop the prunes, and chop the apricots.
Add the chopped fruit to the onion–bacon mixture
with the breadcrumbs, chopped walnuts and parsley,
rosemary and beaten egg.
Season.

Cook the goose

Heat the oven to 180°C/gas 4.
Stuff the goose (not too tightly) and secure with a skewer.
Prick the skin all over to release the fat.
Season and place on a rack in a roasting tin.
Cook for about 1¾ hours, then drain off most of the fat into another tin for the potatoes.
Continue to cook the goose for another 1¼ hours.
Insert a fine skewer into the inner part of a thigh. If the juice runs clear, the bird is cooked.
(Another test is to twist a drumstick: if it moves easily in its socket, the bird is cooked.)
Remove the goose from the roasting tin and leave to rest for at least 20 minutes.

Make the gravy

5 fl oz (150 ml) red wine
8 fl oz (300 ml) chicken stock (see page 6)

Drain the excess fat from the tin.
Add the red wine and the reserved wine from the prunes.
Boil well to reduce.
Add the stock.
Season and boil until the gravy is syrupy.

Pan-fried potatoes

3 lb (1.35 kg) potatoes
salt
black pepper
fat from goose
2–3 sprigs thyme

Peel the potatoes.
Slice to one-eight of an inch (4 mm) thick.
Season with salt and pepper.
Place the tin with the excess goose fat over direct heat.
Add the thyme followed by the potato slices.
Turn and mix the potatoes to coat well with fat.
Roast at 180°C/gas 4 for 30–40 minutes, turning occasionally.

Pineapple with Kirsch (see page 95)

Bread sauce

12 cloves	Push the cloves into the peeled onion.
½ onion	Place in a saucepan with the milk and bring slowly to
15 fl oz (425 ml) milk	the boil. Remove the onion and reserve.
3 oz (75 g) fresh white	Pour the milk on to the breadcrumbs and return to
breadcrumbs	the pan. Cook very gently until thick and creamy.
3 fl oz (75 ml) cream	Return the onion.
salt	Add the cream, seasoning and nutmeg.
black pepper	Bring back to the boil, remove from the heat and
freshly grated nutmeg	cover. When ready to serve, remove the onion and
	reheat gently, adding a little more cream or milk if
	necessary.

Parsnip and apple purée

2 lb (900 g) parsnips	Peel and slice the parsnips and apples.
1 lb (450 g) Bramley	Cook in a little water with the lemon juice and salt
apples	until soft. Drain.
juice of ½ lemon	Work to a purée.
½ tsp salt	Season. Whisk in the butter and cream.
black pepper	If you make the purée the day before, don't add the
1 oz (25 g) butter	butter and cream until just before serving.
2 fl oz (55 ml) cream	

Glazed beetroot

2 lb (900 g) beetroot	Boil the beetroot whole and unpeeled in plenty of
2 oz (50 g) butter	water for about 40 minutes or until tender.
2–3 tblsp sugar	Cool. Peel and remove the root.
zest and juice of 2	Cut the flesh into matchsticks.
oranges	(Use a knife and fork to avoid staining your hands.)
5 fl oz (150 ml) red	Combine the beetroot with the butter, sugar, orange
wine	juice, zest, wine and seasoning.
salt, black pepper	Simmer for 10–15 minutes.
½ tsp allspice	Serve hot.

Gorgonzola cheese

As a change from Stilton, try serving this famous Italian cheese with fruit and nuts. Gorgonzola has a smooth, buttery texture and a firm but creamy consistency. Look for a piece which is creamy in colour, apart from the veins, and smooth. The unevenness of the veining is a characteristic and not a fault.

Christmas pudding with brandy sauce

Make the pudding

7 oz (200 g) butter
3 medium eggs
zest and juice of 1 orange
zest and juice of 1 lemon
10 fl oz (275 ml) stout
5 fl oz (150 ml) sherry
4 oz (100 g) self-raising flour
4 oz (100 g) fresh breadcrumbs
4 oz (100 g) ground almonds
6 oz (175 g) sultanas
6 oz (175 g) raisins
6 oz (175 g) cherries
1 oz (25 g) angelica
2 oz (50 g) dried apricots
2 oz (50 g) whole almonds
8 oz (50 g) dates

Take two 2 pints (1 litre) pudding bowls.
Using about an ounce (25 g) of butter, grease the insides of the bowls thoroughly.
Grate the remaining butter. Beat the eggs.
Finely grate the orange and the lemon.
Mix the zests with the fruit juices, stout and sherry.
Combine the dry ingredients.
Add the sultanas, raisins, cherries, chopped angelica, apricots and dates, the whole almonds and the butter.
Mix in the stout mixture and the beaten eggs.
Spoon into the pudding bowls.
Cover with greaseproof paper and foil or lids.
Place in saucepans with 2–3 inches (5–10 cm) of water, or in a steamer.
Cook for 3 hours at this stage, topping up the water as necessary.
Store in a cool dry place until ready to complete the boiling on the day of serving.
One pudding will serve about ten people. The other can be kept (for up to three months) for another occasion.
Boil for a further 1½ hours on the day of serving.

Make the brandy sauce

4 egg yolks
4 tblsp caster sugar
2 tblsp brandy
5 fl oz (150 ml) white wine
5 fl oz (150 ml) cream

In a heatproof bowl, combine the egg yolks and sugar with the brandy and wine.
Whisk over hot water until thick and mousse-like.
Remove from the heat and whisk until cold.
Whisk the cream and fold in.
Chill.

To serve

2 tblsp brandy or whiskey

Turn out the pudding on to a serving plate. Warm two tablespoons of brandy or whiskey in a saucepan, pour over the pudding and flame. Serve immediately with the brandy sauce.

WINES

First course: *Champagne* brut *(France)*

Labels
Any of the non-vintage Grandes Marques such as Laurent-Perrier, Moët & Chandon *or* G. H. Mumm, Reims.

Availability
Widely available.

Drink
As young as possible.

Serve
Serve cool. Place in the fridge for a couple of hours. Don't forget to keep the bottle cool after opening. For a large gathering try buying magnums, which contain two bottles.

Taste
The beads of bubble are tiny and delightful to watch as they rise to the surface. The heady aromas of fragrant floral tones are enticingly overlaid with toast. A bone dry elegant finish encourages another sip.

Awareness
Produced in northern France, Champagne is a sparkling wine made by blending up to forty different wines from the area known as Champagne, which is also the appellation. It is produced by the 'méthode

champenoise' (also known as the 'traditional method'). It involves several detailed processes, with the second fermentation taking place in bottle. Regulations govern all aspects of Champagne, from permitted grape varieties (chardonnay, pinot noir, pinot meunier) to vineyard location on designated sites.

First course: Chablis AOC (France)

Labels	La Chablisienne *or* Labouré-Roi.
Availability	Widely available.
Drink	2 years old.
Serve	Serve cooled straight from the fridge or cool quickly by plunging in ice and water for 8 minutes.
Taste	Chablis without oak influence (traditional) is very pale with glints of green. Bone dry yet with lean fruit to balance the steely finish.
Awareness	Chablis falls into several quality categories. The biggest production is straightforward AOC Chablis. This is followed by the Premier Cru and Grand Cru wines. For a more complex wine worthy of special occasions try one of the seven Grand Crus: Blanchot, Bougros, Les Clos, Grenouilles, Preuses, Valmur and Vaudésir.
Options	Shippers: Moreau et Fils, Domaine Laroche, Joseph Drouhin. Individual estates: Domaine Alain Geoffroy, William Fèvre, Jean Dauvissat.

Main course: Côte de Beaune Villages AOC (France)

Labels	Louis Latour *or* Moreau Fontaine *or* Bichot.
Availability	Fairly available.
Drink	4 years old.
Serve	Open one hour before serving at room temperature.
Taste	The wine, with its pale ruby colour, is all about strawberry fruits. The initial taste of delicious ripe fruit broadens out and is cut through by a good bite of acidity and supple tannins with a long savoury finish.

Awareness	Côte de Beaune Villages is produced principally from the pinot noir grape. Top-quality single estates (domaines) and merchants (négociants) dominate the market. It is worth getting to know reliable merchants.
Options	As well as the names mentioned above, look out for Jadot, Faiveley, Antonin Rodet, Lupé-Cholet, Reine Pedauque, Jaffelin *or* Bouchard Père et Fils.

Pudding: Muscat de Beaumes-de-Venise AOC VDN (France)

Labels	Jaboulet *or* Vidal Fleury.
Availability	Widely available.
Drink	2 years old.
Serve	Chilled. Place in the fridge for two hours or chill in ice and water for 8 minutes.
Taste	A honeyed golden dessert wine with a distinct peachy muscat aroma of fresh grapes. Fat and weighty in the mouth with honeyed fruits. A lush sweet high-alcohol finish with good acidity preventing it from becoming cloying.
Awareness	Muscat de Beaumes-de-Venise is not a table wine but a 'vin doux naturel' from the southern Rhône. It is a naturally sweet fortified wine produced from the muscat grape.
Options	Reliable producers such as Chapoutier *or* Pascal.

Directory of Fine Food and Wine Suppliers in Ireland

This directory was compiled to help readers, especially those living outside cities, to find the ingredients and wines included in the menus. In most cases, your local supermarket will stock most of the items on your shoppling list and we have not felt it necessary to list the major supermarket chains. We have listed suppliers whose products and services are known to us personally or have been highly recommended. Those with display entries paid a fee and supplied a description of the product/service provided. We do not claim that the list includes all fine food and wine suppliers in Ireland but we hope that it provides a wide enough coverage to be of real help to readers.

How to use this directory

Suppliers are grouped by category—supermarkets and delicatessens (many of which also supply wine), specialist food shops, wine retailers and wine importers. If you are looking for a particular wine that your local off- licence does not stock try telephoning one of the wine importers listed here and ask for the name of the nearest outlet. Importers are often happy to arrange a special delivery where demand warrants.

CONNAUGHT

Galway

Delicatessens

McCambridge's
38/39 Shop Street (beside Lynch's Castle)
Galway
Telephone (091) 62259/63470
Fax (091) 61726
Open 9 am–6 pm Monday–Friday
9 am–5.30 pm Saturday
Closed Sundays and Bank Holidays
Fine food, fine wine and delicatessen. Large selection of Irish and continental cheeses. In-store bakery, cooked meats, pâté, salads, and a wide range of food and wines from acround the world.

Sean Loughnane Fresh Foods
Forster Court
Galway
Telephone (091) 64437/66403
Fax (091) 65492
Open 8 am–9 pm Monday–Sunday
Closed Christmas Day and
St Stephen's Day
Fresh food hall. Bakery, French bread, homemade scones, fresh cream. Delicatessen, own cooked meats, salad bar (self-service). Hot food, chicken, roast joints of meat. Sandwich bar, meats from our own farm.

Silke & Daughters, Munster Avenue, Galway
Tel (091) 61048
Specialist Food
Fleming's Fish Shop, 29 Lr Dominick St, Galway
Tel (091) 66673
Salt Lake Manor Salmon and Seafood, Clifden,
Co Galway Tel (095) 21278

Leitrim

Specialist Food
Eden Plants (herbs), Rossinver, Co Leitrim
Tel (072) 54122

Mayo

Delicatessen
T. McGrath, O'Rahilly St, Ballina, Co Mayo
Tel (096) 22198

Wine retailer
Padraic Tuffy Ltd, Bohenasup, Ballina, Co. Mayo
Tel (096) 21300

Sligo

Delicatessen
Kate's Kitchen, 24 Market St, Sligo Tel (071) 43022

Specialist Food
Tír na nÓg, Wholefood Shop, Grattan St, Sligo
Tel (071) 62752

LEINSTER

Carlow

Wine Retailer
Tully's Wine Shop, 148 Tullow St, Carlow
Tel (0503) 42660

Dublin City

Delicatessens
Fitzpatrick's, 40a Lower Camden St, Dublin 2
Tel (01) 475 3996
The Gourmet Shop,, 48 Highfield Rd, Rathgar, Dublin 6
Tel (01) 497 0365
Magills, 14 Clarendon St, Dublin 2
Tel (01) 671 3830
The Swedish Food Company, 43 Drury St, Dublin 2
Tel (01) 679 9025 also: 46a Capel St, Dublin 1 and
146a Lr Baggot St, Dublin 2
Specialist Food
The Asia Market, 30 Drury St, Dublin 2
Tel (01) 677 9764
Bretzel Kosher Bakery, 1a Lennox St, Dublin 8
Tel (01) 475 2724
F. X. Buckley Butchers, Chatham St, Dublin 2
Tel (01) 677 1491
Farm Produce, 17 Upper Baggot St, Dublin 4
Tel (01) 668 5596
Fox's Fruit and Vegetables, 49a Main St,
Donnybrook, Dublin 4 Tel (01) 269 2892
Here Today, Fruit and Vegetables, 25 South Anne
St, Dublin 2 Tel (01) 671 1454
Mulloy Fishmongers, 12 Lr Baggot Street, Dublin 2
Tel (01) 676 6133

Gammells Delicatessen and Café
33 Ranelagh
Dublin 6
Telephone (01) 496 2311
Open 9 am-8 pm Monday–Sunday
Closed Christmas
Brendan Gammell (late of McCambridge's)
stocks a wide selection of wines, cheeses, home-
made breads, pies,cakes, smoked salmon, and
salads. Personal service guaranteed. Also tea,
coffee and light lunches.

The Runner Bean, Greengrocer, 4 Nassau St,
Dublin 2 Tel (01) 679 4833

Little Italy
139–140 North King Street
Dublin 7
Telephone (01) 872 5208/873 3935
Fax (01) 873 3299
Open 9 am–5 pm Monday– Friday
10 am–1 pm Saturday
Closed Sundays and Bank Holidays
Italian food emporium with a complete range
of Italian produce, from Parma ham to fresh
pasta, from sun-dried tomatoes to the best
estate bottled olive oil. Also Lavazza coffee and
all that's good in Italian food.

Frank Harrison
Mobile Bar and Wine Service
Dublin City and County
7 Westbourne Road, Dublin 6W
Telephone (01) 490 7876

Douglas Food Co
53 Donnybrook Road, Dublin 4
(opposite rugby grounds)
Telephone (01) 269 4066
Fax (01) 269 4492
Open 10 am–7.30 pm Monday–Friday
9.30 am–6 pm Saturday
Closed Sundays and Bank Holidays
A one-stop shop with a large range of gourmet
take-away dishes both fresh and frozen. Also
desserts, Irish and French farmhouse cheeses,
hormone and steroid-free meats. Wines and
breads. Irish, English, French and Italian
speciality products.

Mortons Supermarket
Dunville Avenue, Ranelagh
Dublin 6
Telephone (01) 497 1254/497 1913
Fax (01) 497 1978
Open 9 am–6.30 pm Monday–Saturday
Closed Sundays and Bank Holidays
Family supermarket. Quality seasonal foods,
fresh meats, seafood and game. Cheese, wines,
wild mushrooms, pickled walnuts, stem ginger,
bitter chocolate and general food merchants.
Full catering service available.

Wine importers
James Adam Vintners, 1 Charleston Rd, Dublin 6
Tel (01) 496 3143

Barry and Fitzwilliam, 50 Dartmouth Sq, Dublin 6
Tel (01) 660 6984/66 Fax (01) 660 0479
Brangan and Co Ltd, 7 Deerpark Ave, Dublin 15
Tel (01) 677 1491
P. Callaghan Wines, 19 Maywood Lawn, Raheny, Dublin 5 Tel (01) 831 1369
Cassidy Wines Ltd, 56 Blackthorn Rd, Sandyford Industrial Estate, Dublin 18 Tel (01) 294 4157
Edward Dillon & Co Ltd, 25 Mountjoy Sq, Dublin1 Tel (01) 836 4399
Fitzgerald and Co, 11–12 Bow St, Dublin 7
Tel (01) 872 5911
Gilbeys of Ireland, Gilbey House, Belgard Rd, Dublin 24 Tel (01) 459 7444
Grants of Ireland, St Lawrence Road, Chapelizod, Dublin 20 Tel (01) 626 4455
Hugan Wines, 21 Idrone Drive, Knocksylon, Dublin 16 Tel (01) 494 5871

Delitalia
Telephone : (01) 285 4216

A new catering and wine service providing for Italian dinner parties in your home. Roberto and Céline Pons (former owners of Il Ristorante of Dalkey) will also provide excellent Italian wines. Opening soon, their new Italian food and wine shop.

Kelly and Co (Dublin), 39 Gardiner St, Dublin 1
  Tel (01) 873 2100

T. P. Reynolds & Co, 50 Pembroke Rd, Dublin 4
  Tel (01) 660 9066/0246

Woodford Bourne, 79 Broomhill Road,j Tallaght,
  Dublin 24 Tel (01) 459 9000

Wine retailers

Findlater's (Wine Merchants) Ltd
The Harcourt Street Vaults
10 Upper Hatch Street
Dublin 2
Telephone (01) 475 1699
Fax (01) 475 2530
Open Monday–Friday 9 am–6 pm
Saturday 10 am–5.30 pm
Closed Sundays and Bank Holidays

Extensive range of quality wines from leading growers around the world in unique setting of our vaults. Regular tastings. Special offers. Findlater's cellar plan. Open to the public.

Cooney's, 197 Harold's Cross Road, Dublin 6W
  Tel (01) 497 1671

Cork's Food and Drink, 116 Terenure Rd North,
  Dublin 6 Tel (01) 490 5624

Deveney's Off-Licence, 31 Main Street, Dundrum,
  Dublin 14 Tel (01) 298 4288

Mitchell's Wine Shop
21 Kildare Street, Dublin 2
(at the side of the Shelbourne Hotel)
Telephone (01) 676 0766
Fax (01) 661 1509
Open 10.30 am–5.30 pm
Monday–Friday(Thursday to 8 pm)
10.30 am–1 pm Saturday
Closed Sundays, Bank Holidays

Over 400 different wines and spirits from 18 different countries. Prices from £3.99. Also olive oil, vinegar, cigars, corporate wine gifts, corkscrews, silver, full catering facilities with glass hire, ice, etc.

Allied Drinks Ltd
East Wall Road
Dublin 1
Telephone (01) 836 6898
Fax (01) 874 3998

Suppliers of fine wines to the licensed trade, including Errazuriz, (Chile) Hardys, (Australia) Laroche, (France) Cooks, (New Zealand) Frescobaldi, (Italy) Olarra, (Spain and Beringer, (California).

James Redmond & Sons

25 Ranelagh Village
Dublin 6
Telephone (01) 496 0552/497 1739
Fax (01) 497 8533
Open 9 am–10.25 pm Monday–Saturday
12.30–2 pm/4 pm–9 pm Sunday
*Large range of wine from all the major
producing countries, plus all leading brands of
beers, spirits and liqueurs, along with a
complete range of pastas and sauces.*

*As well as our extensive range of well-known
fine foods and wines, try our new range
from the prestigious Bordeaux house, Borie-
Manoux, and the stunning wines from
Château de Gourgazaud which have been
so highly acclaimed by the world's top wine
writers.
Try our special offers from the South of France
Merlot £3.99
Chateau de Flaugergues (Rosé) £4.99*

Donnybrook Fair, 89 Morehampton Rd,
Donnybrook, Dublin 4 Tel (01) 668 3556
Foley's Fine Wines, 33a Johnstown Rd, Cabinteely,
Dublin 18 Tel (01) 285 0026
Fax (01) 284 0671
Kelly's Wine Cellar, 39 Phibsboro Rd, Dublin 7

Tel (01) 830 4942
Kelly's Off Licence, Malahide Rd, Artane, Dublin 5
Tel (01) 831 1867 Fax (01) 831 9148
O'Briens Fine Wines, 30–32 Donnybrook Rd
Dublin 4 Tel (01) 269 3033
The Magic Carpet, Cornelscourt, Foxrock,
Dublin 18 Tel (01) 289 5678
Nolan's Supermarket, 49 Vernon Ave, Clontarf,
Dublin 3 Tel (01) 833 8361
Verlings Wines, 360 Clontarf Rd, Dublin 3
Tel (01) 833 1653

The Vintry
Specialists in Wines and Spirits
102 Rathgar Road, Dublin 6
Telephone/Fax (01) 490 5477
Open
10.30 am–10.30 pm Monday–Saturday
12.30 pm–2 pm/4 pm–10 pm Sunday
12 pm–10 pm Bank Holidays
Closed Christmas Day, GoodFriday
*Very extensive range of quality wines. Highly
qualified staff with in-depth knowledge. Full
party service including barman, caterer, kegs,
glasses, ice etc.*

Dublin County

Specialist food
Boswells, (sausages and breads), 11 Sydney Tce,
Blackrock, Co Dublin Tel (01) 288 2237
Monkstown Fine Food Co, (wholefoods and spices), 16a
Monkstown Crescent, Monkstown, Co Dublin
Tel (01) 284 4855
Reinhardts (pork butchers) 13 Patrick St, Dún
Laoghaire, Co Dublin Tel (01) 280 7636

Cavistons Food Emporium

59 Glasthule Road, Sandycove
Dún Laoghaire, Co Dublin
Telephone (01) 280 9120/280 2715
Fax (01) 284 4054 ext 25
Open 9 am–6 pm Monday–Saturday
Closed Sundays and Bank Holidays
An Aladdin's cave of exotic food. Wild
mushrooms, sun-dried tomatoes, olive oils,
balsalmic vinegar etc. Also full range of Irish
and Continental farmhouse cheeses. Full range
of home cooked meats, salami, rare roast beef to
chorizo. Fresh olives and organically grown
vegetables in season. Large range of fresh fish
and shellfish. turbot and halibut to fresh clams
and prawns. Full range of poultry and game.
Home smoked salmon, chicken and duck
breasts. Also suppliers to hotels, restaurants and
catering trade. Contact Peter, Stephen, or Ian.

John O'Reilly Victualler

67 Deerpark Road, Mount Merrion
Co Dublin
Telephone: (01) 288 5832/288 9949
Open 9 am–6 pm Monday–Saturday
Closed Sundays and Bank Holidays
We buy the best young beef still with its fat
covering. We still hang our beef to make sure
you eat tender succulent meals. Traditional
cutting methods combined with modern needs.
Thirty years experience. Full delicatessen
counter, fresh fish daily and a local delivery
service free of charge.

Wine retailers

JC's Supermarket, Swords Shopping Centre,
  Rathkeale, Swords, Co Dublin
  Tel (01) 840 2884

J. Hick & Sons, Butchers

Woodpark, Sallynoggin, Dún Laoghaire,
Co Dublin
Telephone (01) 285 4430
Fax (01) 282 2764
Open 8.30 am–1 pm/2 pm–5.30 pm
Tuesday–Thursday
8.30 am–5.30 pm Friday
8.30 am–5 pm Saturday
Closed Monday, Bank Holidays
Traditional and continental pork butchers,
Kasseler, Bratwurst, smoked puddings,
Leberkas, Aufschnitt, hand-cured bacon as it
used to be, hand-made sausage platters, whole
pig barbecue service.

Jus de Vine, Unit 10, Portmarnock Town Centre,
  Co Dublin Tel (01) 846 1192
McCabes Wine Merchants, 51–55 Mount Merrion
  Ave, Blackrock, Co Dublin Tel (01) 288 2037
O'Lorcain Off Licence, 59 Dublin St, Balbriggan,
  Co Dublin Tel (01)841 2309
Searson Wine Merchants
  6a The Crescent, Monkstown, Co Dublin
  Tel (01) 280 0405

Wine Importers

Febvre & Company Limited, Wholesalers

60 Stillorgan Industrial Park
Blackrock Co Dublin
Telephone (01) 295 9030
Fax (01) 295 9036
Open 9am –5.30 pm Monday–Friday
Wines and speciality spirits, balsamic and fruit
vinegars, olive oil, nut oils, dried mushrooms,
quality cooking chocolate, fruit juices,
traditional French pepper and salt mills

Ecock Wine & Spirits Merchants, Unit 3 Newpark
    Centre, Newtownpark Ave, Blackrock,
    Co DublinTel (01) 283 1664
Jenkinson Wines, 6 Brooklawn Ave, Blackrock,
    Co Dublin Tel (01) 288 3710
Mackenway Distributors, 27 Farmleigh Close,
    Stillorgan, Co DublinTel (01) 288 9010
Remy Ireland Ltd, 101 Monkstown Rd,
    Monkstown, Co Dublin Tel (01) 280 4341
Syrah Wines Ltd, 11 Rowanbyrn, Blackrock,
    Co Dublin Tel (01) 289 3670

Wine Development Board of Ireland

33 Clarinda Park West
Dun Laoghaire, Co Dublin
Telephone (01) 280 4666
Fax (01) 280 7566
Open 9 am–5 pm Monday–Friday
Closed Saturday, Sunday, Bank Holidays
*Established in 1977, the Wine Development
Board was set up to promote the sale, and
increase consumption, of wine in Ireland. The
Board runs a series of certified wine education
courses throughout the country. Detailed
syllabus may be obtained by phoning or
writing to Ms Jean Smullen.*

Kildare

Specialist food
McStay's Butchers, Duke St, Athy, Co Kildare,
    Tel (0507) 31868

Kilkenny

Delicatessen
Shortis Wong Delicatessen, 74 John St, Kilkenny
    Tel (056) 61305

Specialist food

Lavistown Foods
Lavistown, Kilkenny
(turn at the Pike pub on the Carlow Road,
left at the end, house first on left)
Telephone: (056) 65145
Open 9 am–6 pm Monday–Sunday
Closed rarely
*Lavistown cheese—Wensleydale type, crumbly,
low fat, tangy. Wonderful sausages, full of
pork, spice, garlic, salt and nothing else. Free-
range pork, lamb in season.*

Louth

Specialist food
The Continental Meat Centre, 20 Clanbrassil St,
    Dundalk, Co Louth Tel (042) 32829
Wine retailer
Egan's Off Licence , 1 Peter St, Drogheda,
    Co Louth Tel (041) 31810

Westmeath

Wines Direct
Telephone (1800) 579579
Fax (044) 40015
*Fine French wines, personally selected by our
team in France. Delivered nationwide, direct
to your door within 3 working days. Phone for
your catalogue today and mix your own case.
(6/12 bottles)*

Wexford

Specialist food
Atlantis, fish shop, Redmond Rd, Wexford
    Tel (053) 22975

Greenacres, wholefood shop & butcher, 56 North
Main St, Wexford Tel (053) 22975

Wine retailer

Caulfield Supermarket Ltd, 17 Irishtown, New Ross,
Co Wexford Tel (051) 22101

Wicklow

Specialist food

Nature's Gold, wholefood shop, Killincarrig Rd,
Greystones, Co Wicklow Tel (01) 287 6301

The Stone Oven Bakery, 63 Lower Main St,
Arklow, Co Wicklow Tel (0402) 39418

MUNSTER

Clare

Delicatessen

Abbey Meats—The Food Emporium, Abbey St,
Ennis, Co Clare Tel (065) 20554

Wine retailers

Oddfellows Liquor Store, Shannon Knight's Inn,
Shannon Town Centre, Shannon, Co Clare
Tel (061) 361 045

Cork

Delicatessens

Iago, Market Alley, Old English Market, Cork
Tel (021) 277 047

Specialist food

Ballycotton Fish Shop, Main St, Ballycotton,
Co Cork Tel (021) 613122

Field's Supermarket, 26 Main St, Skibbereen,
Co Cork Tel (028) 21400

Hudson's Wholefoods, Main St, Ballydehob,
Co Cork Tel (028) 37211

Manning's Food Emporium, Ballylickey, Co Cork
Tel (027) 50456

Natural Foods, wholefood shop, 26 Paul St, Cork
Tel (021) 277244

O'Flynn's Butchers, 36 Marlborough St, Cork
Tel (021) 275 685/272 195

Rosscarbery Recipes, Rosscarbery, Co Cork
Tel (023) 48407

Twomey's Butchers, 16 Pearse St, Clonakilty,
Co Cork Tel (023) 33365

Ummera Smoked Products, smoked salmon,
Ummera House, Timoleague, Co Cork
Tel (023) 46187 Fax (023) 46419

West Cork Herb Farm, Church Cross, Skibbereen,
Co Cork Tel (028) 22299

Ardrahan Cheese Co Ltd
Kanturk
Co Cork
Telephone (029) 78099
Fax (029) 78136

*Ardrahan cheese is semi-soft cheese with a creamy flavour.
It has a washed rind which matures into a golden colour. Ardrahan cheese is made on the farm from pasteurised milk with vegetarian rennet.*

Wine retailers
Daily's Off Licence, Village Green, Douglas, Cork
    Tel (021) 891 733
Fine Wines Ltd, 64 Patrick St, Cork
    Tel (021) 270 273
Foley's Off Licence, 28 Bridge St, Mallow, Co Cork
    Tel (022) 21480
Galvins, Washington St, Cork Tel (021) 276 314
    Clermont Road, Douglas, Cork
    Tel (021) 291 100
    37 Bandon Rd, Cork Tel (021) 316 098
Wine Fare, 19 Patrick St, Fermoy, Co Cork
    Tel (025) 31031

Wine importers
Barry & Fitzwilliam, Glanmire, Cork
    Tel (021) 821 555
Karwig Wines, officlicence, 62 Lisobourne,
    Carrigaline, Co Cork Tel (021) 372 864

Allied Drinks Ltd
Windsor Hill House
Glounthane Co Cork
Telephone (021) 353 438
Fax (021) 354 362
Suppliers of fine wines to the licensed trade, including Errazuriz, (Chile) Hardys, (Australia) Laroche, (France) Cooks, (New Zealand) Frescobaldi, (Italy) Olarra, (Spain and Beringer, (California).

Kerry

Specialist food
Continental Sausages, Fossa, Co Kerry
    Tel (064) 33069

Wine retailers
Garvey's Off Licence, Dingle, Co. Kerry
    Tel (066) 51397 (shopping centre)
    Tel (066) 51649 (pub, strand)

Limerick

Delicatessen
Ivan's, Caherdavan, Ennis Rd, Limerick
    Tel (061) 455 766

Specialist food

Caragh Catering
(Office) Limerick Food Centre
Raheen
Telephone (061) 00422/(088) 543582
Fax (061) 400422
A first class catering service. In your home, a marquee or at the venue of your choice, we can arrange the finest food, wine and service for your guests.

J & B Sykes, venison, Springfield Castle,
    Drumcollogher, Co Kerry, Tel (063) 83162

Fine Wines Limerick
Vintage House, 48 Roche's St, Limerick
Ambassador Centre, Cork Rd, Dooradoyle,
Limerick
Tel (Roches Street branch only)
(061) 417784 Fax (061) 417276
Opening hours: 9 am–11 pm
Monday–Sunday
Closed Sundays 2–4 pm
*Specialist wine and spirit merchants' shops,
with helpful advice on choosing wine to
accompany food. Party bar service and sale or
return available. Largest selection of keenly
priced wines in the west of Ireland. Superb
wine list.*

Grand Cru Wines Ltd
48 Roches Street
Limerick
Telephone: (061)-417784
Fax (061)-417276
Open 9 am–8 pm
*Direct importers of Australian, Chilean,
Italian, French wines. Full list available.
Agents : Lionel Bruck—Burgundy; Albert
Beslombes—Loire.Specialists in grands crus
and petits châteaux from Bordeaux.*

Tipperary

Specialist food
The Clonmel Organic Market & The Honey Pot,
14 Abbey St, Clonmel, Co Tipperary
Tel (052) 21457

Country Choice
25 Kenyon St Nenagh Co Tipperary
Telephone (067) 32596
Fax (067) 32596
Opening hours 9.30 am–6 pm
Closed Sundays
*Country Choice is one of the best food shops in
the country. Peter and Mary Ward specialise
in Irish cheeses in prime condition. The shop
stocks a large range of excellent homemade
breads, jams, pâtés, and meats.*

Cooleeney Farmhouse Cheese
Moyne, Thurles
Co Tipperary
Telephone (0504) 45112
*Farm made speciality cheese with national and
international awards. Cooleeney is described as
a camembert type of cheese. When mature, it is
a rich, creamy farm product and an essential
part of all good dinner menus.*

Wine retailers
Castlehyperstore, 47 Pearse St, Nenagh,
Co. Tipperary Tel (667) 31444

Lonergan's Off Licence
36 O'Connell St, Clonmel,
Co Tipperary
Telephone (052) 21250
Open 11 am–10.30 pm
Monday–Saturday
12.30 pm–2 pm/5 pm –10.30 pm Sunday
*Extensive range of wines from all wine-
producing countries; large selection of beers,
spirits, liqueurs stocked; parties catered for;
crockery, cutlery, table linen, ice also
available.*

Waterford

Delicatessen

Chapman's Delicatessen, 61 The Quay, Waterford
Tel (051) 74938/76200

Wine retailers

L & N Superstores, Parnell St, Dungarvan, Co.
Waterford Tel (058) 41628

L & N Superstores, Priest's Road, Tramore Co.
Waterford (051) 386 036

ULSTER

Antrim

Delicatessen

Cargoes, 613 Lisburn Rd, Belfast
Tel (0232) 665 451

Specialist food

Asia Supermarket, 189 Ormeau Rd, Belfast BT1
Tel (0232) 326 396

Green's Food Fare, 23 Bow St, Lisburn, Co Antrim
Tel (0846) 662 124/641

Sawers, fishmonger, Unit 7, Fountain Centre,
Belfast BT1 Tel (0232) 322 021

Wysner Meats, Butcher Shop and Restaurant,
18 Ann St, Ballycastle, Co Antrim
Tel (02657) 62372

Wine retailer

Direct Wine Shipments, 5/7 Corporation Square,
Belfast BT1, Tel (0232) 238 700

Supermac, Newtownbreda Shopping Centre,
Saintfield Rd, Belfast BT8 Tel (0232) 491 176

The Wine Gallery, Boucher Rd, Belfast BT12
Tel (0232) 231 231

Cavan

Wine retailer

Patrick Kangley, Main St, Bailieborough, Co Cavan
Tel (042) 65480

Donegal

Specialist food

Seafresh, fishmonger, 6a Railway Rd, Letterkenny,
Co Donegal Tel (074) 26118

Down

Delicatessen

Panini, 25 Church Rd, Holywood, Co Down
Tel (0232) 427 774

Specialist food

David Burns, butcher, 112 Abbey St, Bangor,
Co Down Tel (0247) 270 073

Homegrown, 66b East St, Newtownards, Co Down
Tel (0247) 818 318

Wine retailers

The Ava, offlicence, 132 Main St, Bangor,
Co Down Tel (0247) 465 490

James Nicholson, off-licence, 27a Killyleagh St,
Crossgar, Co Down Tel (0396) 830 091

Fermanagh

Specialist food

L.H. Richardson, butcher, Main St, Lisnaskea, Co
Fermanagh Tel (0356) 721 263

Index

Aligot, 140
almonds
    Almond cake, 42
    Breakfast ring cake, 114
    Pear and almond tart, 87
apples
    Apple sauce, 63
    Parsnip and apple purée, 161
Armagnac, 97
Artichoke purée, 132
asparagus, 63
    Green asparagus feuilleté, 62
    John Dory baked with asparagus, 100
Asti Spumanti DOCG, 83
Australian wine, 26, 51, 77, 142
Avocado salad, 152
Avocado soup, chilled, 105

Bacon en croûte with tarragon sauce, 153
Baked potatoes, 35, 36
baking blind, 16
Balsamic sauce, 34
Banana pastries with caramel sauce, 49
Banyuls AOC, 150
Barbera d'Asti DOC, 43
beans
    Mixed bean salad, 106
    Turkish lamb and bean casserole, 119
Béarnaise sauce, 10
Beaujolais Cru AOC Fleurie, 71
Béchamel sauce, 11

beef
    Medallions, with mushrooms, 93
    Rib of beef with grilled marinated
        vegetables, 139
    stock, 7
Beetroot, glazed, 161
Beurre blanc, 11
black olives, 58
Blackcurrant bavarois, 126
Boilie cheese, 76
Bordeaux AOC, 96–7
Bordeaux Grand Cru Classé Pauillac, 65–6
Brandy sauce, 163
Bread sauce, 161
breads, 13–14
Breakfast ring cake, 114
Breakfast sausages, 113
Brie de Meaux, 64
Broccoli, buttered, 48
Brown soda bread, 13
Bulgarian wine, 37
bulghar, 118
Bulghar pilaff, 119

Cabernet Sauvignon (California), 1
    Reserve (Bulgaria), 37
Californian wine, 27, 102–3, 156
Camembert cheese, 154
Caramel sauce, 49
Carrot and apricot sauce, 144
Cashel Blue cheese, 140

Cava, 115
Celeriac purée, 94
Chablis AOC, 164
Champagne *brut*, 163–4
Chardonnay (Hungary), 37
Châteauneuf-du-Pape 65, 88–9
Cheddar cheese, 36
Cheese pastries with pine nut salad, 99
Chianti Riserva DOCG, 50–1
chicken
    Breast of chicken with peppers, 40
    Chicken with peppers and chorizo, 105
    Grilled chicken breasts with morilles
       sauce, 47
    stock, 6, 7
Chilean wine, 27, 155–6
Chilled avocado soup, 105
Chive mayonnaise, 138
Chocolate cake, 148
Chocolate ice cream, 76
chorizo
    Chicken with peppers and chorizo, 105
Christmas pudding, 162–3
Clafoutis of plums, 133
Coolea cheese, 58, 76
Coolleeney Camembert, 140
corkscrews, 19
Côte de Beaune Villages AOC, 164–5
Côtes du Rhône AOC, 60
courgettes
    Courgette gratin, 57
    Two tone courgettes, 64
Cream cheese filling, 140
Crème brûlée with rhubarb, 59
Crème caramel, 107
Croghan cheese, 48, 140
Cucumbers in cream, 80

Dill sauce, 92
Dried fruit compote, 113

duck
    Glazed duck, 68–9
    Magret of duck with apple, 63
    Tagliatelle with smoked duck, 74
Durras cheese, 58

Farmhouse Cheddar cheese, 36
Feta cheese en papillote, 146
Filo pastries with two sauces, 144–5
Fino sherry, 108
fish, *see also* individual fish
    Kedgeree, 111
    Mousseline of, with beurre blanc, 85
    Ragoût of seafood, 32–3
    stock, 8
fruit. *see also* apples
    Blackcurrant bavarois, 126
    Clafoutis of plums, 133
    Dried fruit compote, 113
    Fruit strudel, 141
    Gooseberry fool, 101
    Summer pudding, 120
Fumé Blanc, 102

game stock, 9
Gammon, baked, 111
Gavi DOC, 60
Gazpacho sauce, 46
gelatine, 126
German wine, 25–6, 115
Gewurztraminer AOC, Alsace, 127
glasses, 19–20
Glazed beetroot, 161
Glazed duck, 68–9
Glazed quail, 85
Goats' cheese salad, 95
goats' cheeses, 48
Goose, roast stuffed, 158–9
Gooseberry fool, 101
Gorgonzola cheese, 162
Grand Cru Bourgeois, 134–5

Grated potato cakes, 48
Green asparagus feuilleté, 62
Green salad, 75, 125
Green salad with mustard dressing, 147
Grilled monkfish with olive oil, 75
Gruyère cheese, 125
Gubbeen cheese, 58

Haddock chowder, smoked, 68
Halumi cheese kebabs, 146
Hazelnut meringue cake, 155
herb cheeses, 76
Hollandaise sauce, 10
Horseradish sauce, 131
Hungarian wine, 37
Hunter Valley Chardonnay, 77

Ice cream, chocolate, 76
Irish cheeses, 140
Italian wine, 24–5, 42–4, 50–1, 60, 83,
    127–8, 134

John Dory baked with asparagus, 100

Kedgeree, 111
Kidney and mushroom salad, 79
Kilshanny cheese, 76
Kirsch, Pineapple with, 95

lamb
    Rack of, with tapénade, 52, 56
    stock, 8
    Turkish lamb and bean casserole, 119
Leek noodles, Scallops with, 130
Linguine with mussels, 39
Mackerel, smoked, 118
Magret of duck with apple, 63
Mango salad, 69
Marinated peppers, 41
mayonnaise, 10
Medallions of beef with mushrooms, 93
Meringue cake, hazelnut, 155
Middle Eastern salad, 120

Milleens cheese, 101
Minervois AOC, 121–2
Mint sorbet, 145
Mixed bean salad, 106
Monkfish, grilled, with olive oil, 75
morilles, 47
Mousseline of fish with beurre blanc, 85
Munster cheese, 81
Muscadet-de-Sèvre-et-Maine *sur lie* 88
Muscat de Beaumes-de-Venise AOC, 165
mushrooms
    morilles, 47
    Mushroom sauce, 93
    Stuffed mushrooms, 112
    Warm kidney and mushroom salad, 79
Mussels, linguine with, 39

nectarines, 41
New Zealand wine, 27, 70–1
nut oils, 33

olives, 58
olive oil, 125
Orange Muscat and Flora, 51
Orange rice, 106
Orvieto Classico Secco DOC, 134
Oysters with spicy sausages, 158

Pan-fried potatoes, 159
Parmesan cheese with nectarines, 41
Parsnip and apple purée, 161
pastry, 15–16
    Bacon en croûte, 153
    Banana pastries with caramel sauce, 49
    Cheese pastries with pine nut salad, 99
    Filo pastries with two sauces, 144–5
    Fruit strudel, 141
    Pear and almond tart, 87
    Salmon mousse in pastry sauce, 92
    Strawberry bande with peach coulis, 81
Pâte brisée, 15
Pâte sucrée, 16

Peach coulis, 81
Pear and almond tart, 87
peppers
    Breast of chicken with with peppers, 40
    Chicken with peppers and chorizo, 105
    Marinated, 41
Periquita, 149–50
Pheasant with horseradish sauce, 131
Pigeon breast with Balsamic sauce, 34–5
pilaff
    Bulghar pilaff, 119
    Spicy rice pilaff, 86
    Wild rice pilaff, 147
Pine nut salad, 99
Pineapple with Kirsch, 95
Pinot Blanc AOC Alsace, 141–2
Pinot Grigio DOC, 42–3
Pinotage, 77
Piped potatoes, 101
Portuguese wine, 25, 121, 149–50
potatoes
    Aligot, 140
    Baked, 34, 35
    Grated potato cakes, 48
    Gratin potatoes, 64
    New potatoes with dill, 80
    New potatoes with sea salt and olive
        oil, 41
    Pan-fried potatoes, 159
    Piped potatoes, 101
    roasted with garlic and herbs, 58
    Spicy potatoes, 154
Pouilly Fumé AOC, 96
prawns
    Sauté of prawns with gazpacho sauce,
    46
Premier Cru Classé Sauternes, 89

Quail, glazed, 85

Rack of lamb with tapénade, 56–7

Ragoût of seafood, 32–3
Ravioli, salmon, 54–5
rhubarb
    Crème brûlée with rhubarb, 59
    Rhubarb and strawberry meringue, 36
Rib of beef with marinated vegetables, 139
rice
    Orange rice, 106
    Risotto of sun-dried tomatoes, 124
    Spicy rice pilaff, 86
    Wild rice pilaff, 147
Riesling d'Alsace AOC, 82
Riesling, 115
Rioja Reserva DOCa, 108–9
Risotto of sun-dried tomatoes, 124
Roast stuffed goose, 158–9
Roasted salmon, 80
Roquefort cheese sauce, 86
Rosé, dry, 149

St Emilion Grand Cru Classé, 83
St Nectaire cheese, 133
St Tola cheese, 48
salads
    Avocado salad, 152
    Goats' cheese salad, 95
    Green salad, 75, 125, 147
    Mango salad, 69
    Middle Eastern salad, 120
    Mixed bean salad, 106
    Pine nut salad, 99
    Tabouleh salad, 69
    Walnut salad, 132
    Warm kidney and mushroom salad, 79
salmon
    Roasted salmon, 80
    Salmon mousse in pastry with dill
        sauce, 92
    Salmon ravioli, 54–5
    Salmon terrine, 138
Sancerre AOC, 50

sauces, 10–12
  how to keep warm, 11
sausages, 113
  Chicken with peppers and chorizo, 105
  Oysters with spicy sausages, 158
Sauté of prawns with gazpacho sauce, 46
Sauvignon Blanc (Chile), 155–6
Sauvignon Blanc (New Zealand), 70–1
Scallops with leek noodles, 130
Scones, wholewheat, 14
Seafood, ragoût of, 32–3
Shiraz, 142
Shortbread, 15
Smoked haddock chowder, 68
Smoked mackerel, 118
Smoked trout mousse, 118
Soda bread, brown, 13
soup
  Haddock chowder, smoked, 68
  Tomato and basil soup, 144
South African wine, 27–8, 77
Spanish wine, 108–9, 115, 149
Spicy potatoes, 154
Spicy rice pilaff, 86
Spinach, tossed, 35
Stir-fried vegetables, 154
stocks, 6–9
strawberries
  Crème caramel and summer fruits, 107
  Rhubarb and strawberry meringue, 36
  Strawberry bande with peach coulis, 81
Stuffed mushrooms, 112
Summer pudding, 120

Tabouleh salad, 69
Tagliatelle with smoked duck, 74

Tapénade, 56
Tarragon sauce, 153
tomatoes
  Risotto of sun-dried tomatoes, 124
  Tomato and basil soup, 144
  Tomato sauce, 12
Trout mousse, smoked, 118
Turkish lamb and bean casserole, 119
Turnip purée, 94

Valpolicella DOC, 127–8
Veal baked with rosemary, 124
vegetable purées, 94
Vegetables, stir-fried, 154
Vin Santo, 44
Vinho Verde DOC, 121

Walnut and treacle bread, 13
Walnut roulade, 70
Walnut salad, 132
Warm kidney and mushroom salad, 79
West Cork cheeses, 58
White bread, 14
Wholewheat scones, 14
Wild rice pilaff, 147
wine, 17–28
  decanting, 22
  equipment, 19–20
  judging, 18–19
  serving, 22
  storage, 20–1
wine labels, 23–8

Yoghurt and cucumber sauce, 144
Yoghurt bowl, 113

Zinfandel (California), 156